Knou

"When these girlfriends get together, God is definitely at the center! Though their voices are distinct, their message and mission are seamless, weaving personal stories, biblical truths, and life-changing application into a truly meaningful devotional. *Knowing God by Name* opens our eyes to the many facets of God's love and mercy, letting us see Him more clearly and know Him more deeply. Well done!"

—Liz Curtis Higgs, author of *The Girl's Still Got It*

"*Knowing God by Name* is a treasure of blessing for us Bible-study junkies. Whether we realize it or not, names are significant, because who we believe we are affects how we respond to life. The same can be said of our Creator: who God says He is affects how He responds to His children. This study takes the reader on a personal and captivating journey through rich, deep layers of God's character, with each one of His names jumping to life off the pages. I would recommend this study to anyone who desires a fresh connection to the One who created and named them."

—Kasey Van Norman, president of Kasey Van Norman Ministries and author of the *Named by God* book and Bible study series

"Sharon, Gwen, and Mary are the real deal—the kind of girlfriends who cause you to lean forward when they start talking about Jesus *and* the kind you want to hang out with at Starbucks after Bible study. Plus, *Knowing God By Name* is a heart-expanding, potentially life-changing, hope-on-steroids subject. Which makes this literary faith adventure a must-read!"

—Lisa Harper, author, Bible teacher, and Women of Faith speaker

"How beautiful is the woman who truly knows God and relies on Him for her strength each day! *Knowing God By Name* brings us into a deeper and richer relationship with Him and helps us grow in our understanding of His attributes. This book takes us on a journey through God's Word to discover the descriptive names of God and recognize what each name means to us personally. A great group study or a refreshing individual read, this book will enrich every woman's intimacy with her heavenly Father."

—Karol Ladd, author of *Positive Life Principles for Women*

"If you long to know God more personally and to understand His character, attributes, and love, read this book! *Knowing God by Name* is a powerful eight-week devotional on the names of God that explores every aspect of His ability to transform your life. This book will give you a fresh understanding of who He really is!"

—Carol Kent, speaker and author of *When I Lay My Isaac Down*

"Not just another study, this is an eight-week adventure in searching out the awe-inspiring, jaw-on-the-floor, blow-us-away character qualities of an all-powerful, everlasting Father. We're talking life-changing stuff here. Not just because it's beautifully written—though, oh my goodness, it certainly is—but because it helps us know our God better. And the more we know Him, the more we know how very safe our faith is when we place it in Him alone. Authentic, touching, personal stories from three of my very favorite authors make the journey to that faith-place even sweeter."

—Rhonda Rhea, radio and TV personality and author of twelve books, including *Espresso Your Faith*

"Knowing God is paramount to everything else in a believer's life. That's why I was excited to read *Knowing God by Name.* This remarkable resource, which provides insight into life's toughest questions and reveals the secrets of God's heart toward you, will take your spiritual relationship to new heights. You may even experience a personal revival. I did."

—Micca Campbell, speaker and author of *An Untroubled Heart*

KNOWING GOD BY NAME

KNOWING GOD BY NAME

SHARON JAYNES
GWEN SMITH
MARY SOUTHERLAND

MULTNOMAH
BOOKS

Knowing God by Name
Published by Multnomah Books
12265 Oracle Boulevard, Suite 200
Colorado Springs, Colorado 80921

Italics in Scripture quotations reflect the author's added emphasis.

Hardcover ISBN: 978-1-60142-469-3
eBook ISBN: 978-1-60142-470-9

Cover design by Kelly L. Howard

Published in the United States by WaterBrook Multnomah, an imprint of the Crown Publishing Group, a division of Random House LLC, New York, a Penguin Random House Company.

Library of Congress Cataloging-in-Publication Data
Jaynes, Sharon.
Knowing God by name : a girlfriends in God faith adventure / Sharon Jaynes, Gwen Smith, Mary Southerland.
pages cm
ISBN 978-1-60142-469-3 (pbk.) — ISBN 978-1-60142-470-9 (electronic)
1. God (Christianity)—Name—Textbooks. 2. Christian women—Religious life—Textbooks. 3. od (Christianity)—Name—Prayers and devotions. 4. Christian women—Prayers and devotions. I. Smith, Gwen, 1970– II. Southerland, Mary. III. Title.
BT180.N2J39 2013
242'.643—dc23
2013015577

Printed in the United States of America
2014

10 9 8 7 6 5 4

Special Sales

Most WaterBrook Multnomah books are available at special quantity discounts when purchased in bulk by corporations, organizations, and special-interest groups. Custom imprinting or excerpting can also be done to fit special needs. For information, please e-mail SpecialMarkets@WaterBrookMultnomah.com or call 1-800-603-7051.

This book is dedicated to our husbands:
Steve Jaynes, Brad Smith, and Dan Southerland—
three of the most precious men God ever created.

Contents

Week 5

Week 6

Week 7

Week 8

Introduction

What's in a Name?

Three Bedouin shepherd boys wandered a hillside near the northwest shore of the Dead Sea, in search of a lost goat. One tossed a rock into the dark opening of a cave, hoping to startle the wayward animal out of hiding. When the rock made contact, what the boys heard was not the muffled sound of a goat's bleat, a ricochet off a cave wall, or even a thump against the hard dusty ground. It was the sound of shattering pottery.

The boys ventured into the cave and discovered there in the Judean desert a cache of mysterious clay vessels stuffed with ancient Hebrew writing—the first of what we've come to know as the Dead Sea Scrolls. Hundreds of jars. Hundreds of scrolls. Thousands of words. Precious parchments rolled up and tucked into clay jars, only to be discovered in 1946, some two thousand years after they were penned. Over the next several years, fifteen thousand fragments were retrieved from eleven different caves.

A few years ago, a museum in my (Sharon's) hometown hosted a traveling exhibit of the Dead Sea Scrolls. I walked into the dimly lit room expecting to look at a piece of history, but I experienced so much more. God's presence was thick. The Holy Spirit hovered close to the writings He had breathed into the writers inspired centuries earlier. My soul was stirred.

Enshrined in glass cases surrounding me were precious ancient parchments. Below each fragment of Hebrew or Aramaic text, the English translations were provided—translations that matched almost perfectly the words in my very own Bible. I was struck by the unchangeable authenticity of God's Word through the centuries. So far, more than 230 biblical texts have been found among the 972 manuscripts, representing every book except Esther. Here was Genesis. Psalms. Isaiah. Deuteronomy. Old friends. Holy words. Unscathed by time. Unchanged by man.

As I stared in awe at one particular scroll fragment from the book of Deuteronomy, I noticed four dots where the Hebrew letters for *Yahweh* should have appeared. Four dots. Then I saw it again in the book of Isaiah: "In the wilderness prepare the way of • • • •" (Isaiah 40:3, ESV).

And then it hit me just how deeply the scribes reverenced and revered the name YHWH. They wouldn't say the Name. They wouldn't even write the Name. And yet YHWH is the name that God said would be remembered from generation to generation (Exodus 3:15). And while God is exceedingly holy, He is also intimately personal. He reminded Moses, "I am...the God of Abraham,...Isaac and...Jacob" (verse 6).

And, friend, He is the God of Sharon, Gwen, Mary—and you!

Infinitely holy. Intimately personal. Our God wants not only to be worshiped but to be known. In 1 Chronicles 16:10–11, David urged his people:

> Glory in his holy name;
> let the hearts of those who seek the LORD rejoice.
> Look to the LORD and his strength;
> seek his face always.

What's in a Name?

Of course, if we're to "glory in his holy name," it makes sense that we'll need to know what that name is. In the Old Testament, the Israelites were surrounded by cultures that worshiped a variety of gods with many different names. However, the one true God made it clear that He alone is to receive our worship. "Hear, O Israel: The LORD our God, the LORD is one," the Shema begins (Deuteronomy 6:4). And while He is one God, He has many names.

In the sixty-six books of the Bible that were written over approximately fifteen hundred years, God revealed various names that reflect His multifaceted character and infinitely diverse ways. To the outcast Hagar, He was El Roi, the God Who Sees. To the needy Abraham, He was Yahweh Yireh, the Lord Will Provide. To the rock-toting teen warrior David, He was El Shaddai, the All-Sufficient One. In each of these instances, God revealed a new aspect of His being to show that He was sufficient to take care of every need, all powerful to take care of every foe, and all present to take care of every circumstance.

In ancient times names carried powerful significance. In addition to distinguishing one person from another and connecting family members, names were thought to reflect a person's character, nature, and destiny. Joseph's two sons were named Manasseh, meaning "God has made me forget all my trouble and all my father's household," and Ephraim, meaning "God has made me fruitful in the land of my suffering" (Genesis 41:50–52). Abraham's name meant a "father of many nations," and the name of his wife, Sarah, meant "princess—the mother of many nations"[1] (Genesis 17:5, 15–16). Then there was Jacob, whose name meant "trickster," Esau whose name meant "red," and Jabez whose name meant "pain." If you're familiar with their lives, you can see how these names are intricately connected with each person's story.

God has many names in the Bible, and just like the names of the people to whom He revealed Himself, each one brings to light something about His character and His ways—who He is and what He does. Our finite human minds can barely comprehend even a fraction of the depth of His wisdom, the breadth of His love, the magnitude of His power, or the height of His grace. But like a multifaceted diamond, each name invites us to glory in a different aspect of our amazing God.

Knowing God Intimately

In the pages to follow, we'll introduce you to forty different names and attributes of God. But we don't want you to simply know God's names. We want you to know God Himself—on a personal level. We want you to call Him by name and to call *on* Him by name. And you can be sure of this: He knows your name...He calls your name. I love God's promise to us: "Do not be afraid, for I have ransomed you. I have *called you by name;* you are mine" (Isaiah 43:1, NLT).

Our purpose is not to cover every name of God mentioned in the Bible or to study every theological nuance of the names we do cover. Rather, we long for you to draw closer to the heart of God by gaining new insights as to who God is and what He does on your behalf. We pray that as you reflect on the various names of God, you will experience Him in fresh ways and with deeper intimacy.

We hope you read our previous Girlfriends in God book, *Trusting God.* It's the perfect introduction to this study. These two books are knit together with the purpose of drawing you closer to God. We believe the more you know Him, the more you'll trust Him. Isaiah wrote, "Let him who walks in the dark, who has no light, *trust in the name of the LORD* and rely on his God" (Isaiah 50:10). The psalmist wrote, "Those who know your name will trust in you, for you, LORD, have never forsaken those who seek you" (Psalm 9:10). Oh, girlfriend, you can know God by name and you can trust Him.

For most of the names of God, we'll include the Old Testament Hebrew or Aramaic or the New Testament Greek rendering of the name as well as the English translation. Just as in our Girlfriends in God online devotions, we'll include Today's Truth—a Bible verse in which the name is used. And each devotional closes with a prayer. For Day 6 of each week, we've provided questions to help you reflect more deeply and personally on the five names or attributes covered in that particular week. We encourage you to gather a group of girlfriends into a GiG group and study the names together. We know from our own friendship that there's so much to be gained by sharing with one another what you're discovering about God. In fact, the three of us have created free online videos for each week, and we'd love to join you in this study. So grab a cup of coffee, click on www.girlfriendsingod.com, and find us on the Knowing God by Name page.

So let's get started! We can hardly wait to hear what God reveals to you as you open the treasure chest of His Word and begin to know God by name.

Girlfriends IN GOD

Sharon Jaynes, Gwen Smith, and Mary Southerland

The people who know their God will display strength and take action. (Daniel 11:32, NASB*)*

Day 1

The Creator
Elohim

Sharon Jaynes

Today's Truth

In the beginning God [Elohim] created the heavens and the earth. (Genesis 1:1)

Friend to Friend

Elohim is the first name for God in the Bible, and it is found in the first sentence of God's Word. "In the beginning God [Elohim] created the heavens and the earth" (Genesis 1:1). So let's begin our journey of knowing God by name...in the beginning.

Before the creation of the world, there was nothing. Our human minds can't even conceive or imagine *nothing.* But into the nothing God spoke, and what was not became what is.

When God hung the sun in the morning sky and the moon in the inky expanse, when He sprinkled the stars to dance in the night, when He separated the waters of heaven from the waters of the earth, when He shaped the dry land, scattered seed for vegetation, stocked the seas with marine life, and filled the skies with winged fowl, He did so with words. "And God said, 'Let there be,'" and it was so (verses 3, 6, 14). "By the word of the LORD were the heavens made, their starry host by the breath of his mouth" (Psalm 33:6).

But on the sixth day, God did a little something different. "Then God said, 'Let Us make man in Our image, according to Our likeness'" (Genesis 1:26, NASB).

So the holy hand of God reached down, gathered dust from the ground, and with sacred fingertips formed man. He then leaned over the lifeless form and "breathed into his nostrils the breath of life, and the man became a living being" (Genesis 2:7).

After each of the first five days of creation, as the sun set over the horizon, God said, "It is good." Six times, at the end of each phase of His handiwork, He reiterated His approval. In reading the story, we ride the rhythm of repetition only to be brought to a sudden halt by the Creator's words when He looked at the lone man with no suitable companion: "It is *not* good for the man to be alone" (Genesis 2:18).

> So the LORD God caused a deep sleep to fall upon the man, and he slept; then He took one of his ribs and closed up the flesh at that place. The LORD God fashioned into a woman the rib which He had taken from the man, and brought her to the man. (Genesis 2:21–22, NASB)

Actor and author Bruce Marchiano paints a beautiful picture of God fashioning Eve.

> He shapes her frame and shades her skin. He molds her mind and measures her stature. He sculpts the contour of her face, the almonds of her eyes, and the graceful stretch of her limbs. Long before she has even spoken a word, he has held her

> voice in his heart, and so he ever-so-gently tunes its timbre. Cell by cell, tenderness by tenderness, and with care beyond care, in creation he quite simply *loves her.*[2]

Eve was the "crowning touch of God's creative masterpiece and the inspiration of man's first poetry."[3] She was not an afterthought, but God's grand finale—His magnificent masterpiece. God concluded the first week of the world's existence, and the curtain fell with the words: "God saw all that he had made, and it was *very* good" (Genesis 1:31).

Now let's take a closer look at the very first name of God found in the Bible: Elohim. The Hebrew word *Elohim* is the plural form of the Hebrew word *El,* one of the oldest designations for divinity. It means "mighty one or strong one."[4] The name Elohim encapsulates the truth of God's creative power, majesty, and might, as well as His sovereign rule over all creation. The fact that it is the plural form of El points to the truth of the Trinity—God in three persons: Father, Son, and Holy Spirit. They are the collective Us in Genesis 1:26. Elohim is used over two thousand times in the Old Testament to name God, and thirty-two of those occur in Genesis 1:1–2:3.

Knowing God as Elohim answers three big questions all of us face: *Who am I? Where did I come from? Why am I here?*

Who are you? You are an image bearer of God. Elohim said, "Let Us make man in Our image." And then, "Male and female He created them" (Genesis 1:26–27, NASB).

Where did you come from? God fashioned you, formed you, and created your inmost being. David wrote:

> For you created my inmost being;
> you knit me together in my mother's womb.

I praise you because I am fearfully and wonderfully made;
your works are wonderful,
I know that full well.
My frame was not hidden from you
when I was made in the secret place.
When I was woven together in the depths of the earth,
your eyes saw my unformed body.
All the days ordained for me were written in your book
before one of them came to be. (Psalm 139:13–16)

Why are you here? You were created for God and to glorify God (Isaiah 43:7), because it pleased Him to do so (Ephesians 1:5). The concept of glory can be difficult to wrap our human minds around. Simply put, *God's glory* is how He makes His presence known. You, my friend, are a platform from which God displays His magnificence and makes His presence easy to see.

Knowing you were created *by* God and *for* God confirms that you have great value and great purpose, regardless of how you feel about yourself, regardless of how you came into this world, regardless of what others have said about you in the past. Every human life is sacred, no matter how it began.

Now let me go a little deeper. As you ponder God's speaking the universe into existence, do you think anything in your life is too difficult for Him to take care of? Any problem too complex for Him to solve? Any illness beyond His power to heal? Any child too rebellious for Him to tame? Any marriage too far gone for Him to restore? Oh, sister, nothing is impossible for Elohim, the mighty Creator. He can breathe life into any seemingly hopeless situation that comes your way. "For nothing is impossible with God" (Luke 1:37, NLT). You can depend on Elohim to weave a design out of the tangled circumstances of your life, even when they seem as shapeless and dark as the earth prior to His first utterance of "Let there be."

Let's Pray

Elohim, mighty Creator, I praise You that You spoke, and what was not became what is. From the minutia of an atom to the grandness of the sea, the whole earth shouts the truth of Your creative glory. I thank You for Your mighty power that can create order from my chaos, fashion beauty from my brokenness, and bring light into the darkness of my world. I rest assured that nothing is too hard for You to handle. In Jesus's name, amen.

The Everlasting God
El Olam

Gwen Smith

Today's Truth

Abraham planted a tamarisk tree in Beersheba and called there on the name of the Lord, the Everlasting God. (Genesis 21:33, esv)

Friend to Friend

My curiosity begs to understand life. My mind longs for logic. I am not overly fond of ungraspable concepts. When I was a child, I asked a million questions. *Why is the sky blue? Are angels all men? Why do bad things happen? Why can't we send my brussels sprouts to the starving children in Africa? Who created God?*

I wanted answers.

I still do.

Give me a story that grabs my attention at the beginning. Fill it with intrigue. Throw in some high conflict and drama in the middle, and then catch the bad guys, tie up the loose ends, and call it done. Cue the applause. Strike up the band! Bring down the curtain. But don't even think about leaving me hanging...and certainly don't ask me to *tune in next week* for the missing story-pieces.

Now that you are clued in to a bit of my "crazy," you can imagine how I reacted as a youngster when the concept of infinity was introduced in math class. Suit me up in a straitjacket and take me to a rubber room. I thought my math teacher was nuts. *You mean I'm supposed to comprehend, work with, and accept something that has no beginning and no ending? Really? That's not neat. It's not simple. It makes my brain hurt to even think about it!*

Pure frustration, packaged in a sideways figure eight.

A mind-maddening math mystery.

Infinity.

Once I rose above the psychological drama-trauma of this new math concept, I figured out how to solve problems with infinity, even though I couldn't wrap my brain around it. I completed my homework assignments and passed the tests—without running my fingernails down the chalkboard in a defiant, adolescent tantrum of revolt. Miracle.

Despite my coming to terms with infinity, God's eternal nature is one of several divine characteristics that I find difficult to grasp. As much as my inner four-year-old would like it to, the Bible does not begin with "Once upon a time," and it does not end with "And they all lived happily ever after." The love saga of God, written in crimson by Christ, is a mystery that began before the dawn of time and continues forever. God's existence transcends space, matter, and time.

Let the reality of the Everlasting God blow your mind for a minute…

> Behold, God is great, and we know him not;
> the number of his years is unsearchable. (Job 36:26, ESV)

Have you not known? Have you not heard?
The LORD is the everlasting God,
the Creator of the ends of the earth.
He does not faint or grow weary;
his understanding is unsearchable. (Isaiah 40:28, ESV)

God is God.

He is great.

Unsearchable.

There is no one like Him, not one. Not now. Not ever. He is uniquely and mysteriously eternal. In Genesis 21:33, we read, "Abraham planted a tamarisk tree in Beersheba and called there on the name of the LORD, the Everlasting God" (ESV). Abraham called out to El Olam—the Everlasting God. As we discussed yesterday, *El* is the ancient Hebrew designation for "mighty one." *Olam* means "world, universe, everlasting time or space."[5] God's existence cannot be featured on a time line because it does not come neatly packaged with a clearly defined beginning and ending. In fact, He *is* the Beginning and the End, the Alpha and Omega, the First and the Last.

Moses also referred to the eternal nature of God. Just before he died, Moses called God Elohei Kedem, the Hebrew name that means "eternal God," when he handed out blessings of strength and security to the people of the tribe of Asher.

There is no one like the God of Israel.
He rides across the heavens to help you,
across the skies in majestic splendor.
The eternal God is your refuge,
and his everlasting arms are under you.
(Deuteronomy 33:26–27, NLT)

I would guess that, like me, you love the thought of God as your refuge. My heart completely resonates with the concept of His everlasting arms beneath me. Holding me. Protecting me. Guiding me. Do I fully understand it? Not at all. But it sure does help me accept the concept of God's eternal nature, helping ground my experience of this mind-blowing truth in something tangible.

When we invite the One who is beyond space, matter, and time into *our* space, matter, and time, we position ourselves to experience El Olam as a refuge for all eternity. You and I run out of energy. We grow weary. We lose heart. God *never* does. The everlasting God does not faint or grow weary, and when we call out to Him, He renews our strength and revives our hope.

The Bible pulls back the curtain of eternity in the book of Revelation to give us a glimpse of what forever looks like. Do you realize what's going on before the throne of God in heaven right now? Unparalleled worship. Celestial creatures with massive amounts of eyes and wings—strangely foreign to us, but at home in the sacred throngs of heaven—surround the throne, raising their voices to exalt the everlasting God. Day and night they never cease to declare,

> Holy, holy, holy, is the Lord God Almighty,
> who was and is and is to come! (Revelation 4:8, ESV)

Yeah. I'm the girl who wants life to make sense, but I've been learning that there are some things in life that we just need to accept rather than understand. Things we need to take at face value…at *faith* value. For me, this is one of them. I worship El Olam—who was and is and is to come. Infinite grace. I don't need to know how God's eternal nature works to believe it is at work in our world and in my circumstances. I'm so grateful that on the day my lungs exhale my final earthly breath and my eyes lift to see Jesus face to face, all my questions will be not only satisfied, but also forgotten. Not just for a moment, but for all eternity.

> You keep him in perfect peace
> whose mind is stayed on you,
> because he trusts in you.
> Trust in the LORD forever,
> for the LORD GOD is an everlasting rock.
> (Isaiah 26:3–4, ESV)

Let's Pray

Heavenly Father, El Olam, Everlasting God, You surely are great! You are the most amazing mystery I will ever know. Help me to trust You, beyond my understanding. Increase my faith, and help my life to reflect Your infinite grace. In Jesus's name, amen.

Day 3

The Lord My Rock
Yahweh Tsuri

Mary Southerland

Today's Truth

The Lord is my rock, my fortress and my deliverer; my God is my rock, in whom I take refuge. He is my shield and the horn of my salvation, my stronghold. (Psalm 18:2)

Friend to Friend

Through the years, the mountains of North Carolina have been a favorite vacation spot for our family. I recall one summer in particular when our son, Jered, was nine and our daughter, Danna, was six. We had heard so much about Grandfather Mountain and decided the kids were finally old enough to handle the physical demands of such an adventurous climb. Our excitement grew as our faithful old van wound its way up the mountain to the visitor center. The kids jumped out, yelling for us to hurry, ready for the adventure to begin!

The first leg of the expedition required us to cross a high, swinging bridge to enjoy the most spectacular view offered by Grandfather Mountain. With the confidence of veteran climbers, we traipsed across the bridge with ease and in absolute awe of the mountainous beauty. None of us really wanted to move from our scenic overlook, but when the crowd grew larger and the cold winds started picking up, we decided it was time to go. Reluctantly, we began walking back to the van. Then we spotted the sign pointing to hiking trails just ahead—and we love to hike—so we decided to try out a few trails.

At the starting point of the climb, we saw a large wooden billboard warning all hikers to make sure they were fully equipped for the trails ahead, listing necessities like water, food, hiking gear, and first-aid kits. When I pointed out the sign to my husband, he said, "Honey, that sign is *not* for Southerlands!" Of course! What was I thinking?

After sauntering past the billboard, we embarked on what seemed to be a pleasantly easy climb. Soon we came to an ambiguous fork in the path. There were no maps or signs and not a single person to guide us. As we were contemplating which path to take, a group of college students came rambling down one of the mountain paths, laughing and chattering about the "excellent" climb they had just made. We asked if the trail they had just taken would be easy enough for the kids. Assessing our young children clad in shorts, T-shirts, and newly purchased slip-on sneakers, accompanied by their two ill-equipped parents, the students assured us we could handle the hike with no problems at all. Off we went!

It wasn't long before we realized we were in serious trouble. The path grew harder and steeper. We met fewer and fewer climbers until it seemed as if we were the only ones left on the mountain. I do remember thinking, *Now tell me again, God,* why *I married this man!* Of course, I knew why. It was just a momentary lack of resolve brought on by the increasing panic.

On we climbed, scaling huge boulders, plastering ourselves against massive rocks as we found ourselves on an extremely narrow path that skirted a deadly drop of several hundred feet. At one point,

Dan and I were literally grasping our children's feet and planting them in safe places, holding them steady in order to prevent a fall off the mountain. We could not turn around. The paths were so steep that our only option was to climb over the mountaintop and make our way down the other side. With every step my alarm grew until we rounded the last curve and found ourselves looking at the highest point of the mountain. It was a breathtaking view and a terrifying prospect all in one, because one last boulder loomed in front of us—the biggest one of all. As we drew closer, that boulder became a thing of beauty! Someone had been there before us and bolted metal stakes into the side of the boulder, forming a ladder we could use to scale that massive rock and reach the other side and the path that would take us safely down the mountain. We finished the climb, realizing that God does indeed take care of the faithful and the foolish, as well as those of us who vacillate in between.

As we were driving home, the perfect provision of God swept over me in sweet relief. Just as surely as God took care of us on that mountain, He takes care of us every minute of every day. God truly is our Rock—our Yahweh Tsuri.

The Bible is filled with references to God as a rock. The Hebrew noun *tsur* is often translated "rock" or "stone," while *petra* is the Greek word for "rock." The ancient writers emphasized this aspect of God for good reason. Rocks provided shade and shelter in the wilderness and were used to create altars, temples, houses, and city walls. Piles of stones memorialized important events in Israel's history. What's more, God's commandments, given to Moses, were etched on stone so that all generations would learn His Law. The word *rock* epitomizes God's persistent faithfulness.

I can't think of a better word than *rock* to represent God's nature and character. He is faithful and His love endures forever. His presence offers protection and shelter from the storms of life. When we pray to the Lord our Rock, we are conversing with the never-changing God whose purposes and plans remain fixed and steadfast. The New Testament identifies Jesus as the spiritual rock that accompanied the Israelites during their challenging journey through the desert (1 Corinthians 10:4). He is also the stone the builders rejected but which has become the very cornerstone upon which God's church is built (Acts 4:10–11; Ephesians 2:20–21).

I first realized just how precious Yahweh Tsuri was and would be in my life when I found myself at the bottom of a dark and lonely pit called clinical depression. My world simply crumbled around me. Everything I had counted on my whole life suddenly seemed uncertain, even my faith in God. How had He let me fall into this pit? I had no idea how I had gotten to such a desolate place, and even more frightening, I had no idea how to get out. I cried out to Him with a desperation I had never experienced before—and let me tell you, I was no stranger to desperate times. My life story includes an alcoholic father, a poverty-ridden childhood, a mother who battled cancer, being molested as a teenager, a struggle with infertility, the stress of ministry, the anxiety of my husband's heart problems...the list of crises I've encountered is formidable. Yet depression and its threat to smother my faith was worst of all. While I sat at the bottom of that pit, God gave me the promise of Psalm 40, a promise that redefined my very being and formed the foundation for the life and ministry He has given me today.

> I waited patiently for the LORD;
>   he turned to me and heard my cry.
> He lifted me out of the slimy pit,

out of the mud and mire;
he set my feet on a rock
and gave me a firm place to stand. (verses 1–2)

When the storms of life come, as they surely will, and when the world around us begins to tremble, as it inevitably will, we need not be shaken. The Lord who is the Rock eternal will be there, giving us a firm place to stand.

God is faithful and He proves that promise to us over and over again. "For the LORD is good; his steadfast love endures forever," the psalmist proclaims (Psalm 100:5, ESV). If God came through yesterday, He will come through today. If God was faithful yesterday, He will be faithful today. His love never changes, He holds each tomorrow in the palm of His hand, and He has gone before us, through the darkness of every trial and over each mountain erected by the circumstances of life, making a way.

Rejoice, girlfriend! Your faith's firm foundation is the Lord your Rock—your Yahweh Tsuri.

Let's Pray

Father, You are my Rock. When I can count on nothing else in this world, I can count on You to be my shelter, my strength, and my peace. Help me remember and celebrate each victory You have accomplished in my life. I stand in Your power alone, Lord, and declare my faith in You, Yahweh Tsuri, my Rock and my Redeemer. In Jesus's name, amen.

Day 4

The All-Sufficient One
El Shaddai

Sharon Jaynes

Today's Truth

I am God Almighty [El Shaddai]; walk before me and be blameless. I will confirm my covenant between me and you and will greatly increase your numbers. (Genesis 17:1–2)

Friend to Friend

I was exhausted. I was drenched in sweat. I was filled with an inexplicable joy like I had never known before. It was the day Steven Hugh Jaynes Jr. emerged from the cozy confines of my womb and made his grand debut into the world.

Before my son was born, I never knew so much love could be wrapped in one tiny package. After twenty-three and a half hours of pushing and pulling, heaving and ho-ing, he finally decided to leave his comfy sauna and face the bright lights of the delivery room. As soon as the umbilical cord was severed, the nurses whisked him away to make sure ten fingers and toes were accounted for, wrap him in a cozy blanket, and place a cap on his fuzzy head.

We got to visit for a little while, this new little person and I, but alas they needed to run a few more tests to make sure all was well. A short time later, a nurse brought my little man to my room, placed the squirmy bundle on my chest, and smiled. Steven's head bobbed about like he was looking for something. He whimpered. He searched. And then he found what he was rooting for. Steven latched on to my body, and the miracle began. Nourishing, life-giving sustenance began to flow. And for the first time, I truly understood the name El Shaddai.

One of the names of God in the Old Testament is El Shaddai. We've already seen that the word *El* means "mighty" or "strong." *El Shaddai* is often translated "God Almighty," "God, the powerful one," or "God, the mighty one."[6] *Shaddai* comes from the Hebrew root word *shad,* meaning "breast." It gives us a wonderful picture of God as "the One who nourishes, supplies, and satisfies."[7]

The word *Shaddai* describes power, but not in the usual thunder-and-lightning sense. This is the power to nourish, to sustain life, to quiet one's longings. God's name El Shaddai is used forty-eight times in the Old Testament, thirty-one of those occurring in the book of Job.

The Hebrew root word *shad* may seem an odd choice for referring to God. But if you have ever held a hungry, crying, restless, or anxious babe in your arms and then witnessed the calm that sweeps over him when placed to his mother's breast, you understand. The crying ceases, the restlessness calms, the hunger is satisfied, and anxiousness melts away. And to that child, the mother from whom life-giving, soul-satisfying nourishment flows seems all powerful. What a beautiful image of our God who satisfies our every need, calms our every fear, and soothes our every longing.

We see the all sufficiency of God's power on display throughout Scripture. In Genesis 12:1–3, God gave Abram an incredible promise.

> The LORD had said to Abram, "Leave your country, your people and your father's household and go to the land I will show you.
>
> "I will make you into a great nation
> and I will bless you;
> I will make your name great,
> and you will be a blessing.
> I will bless those who bless you,
> and whoever curses you I will curse;
> and all peoples on earth
> will be blessed through you."

But time passed, and Abram and his wife Sarai had no children, no heir. When Abram was ninety-nine years old, and Sarai was eighty-nine, God came to him once again and reiterated His promise. In this scene we find the first declaration of His name El Shaddai.

> I am God Almighty [El Shaddai]; walk before me and be blameless. I will confirm my covenant between me and you and will greatly increase your numbers. (Genesis 17:1–2)

God then changed Abram's name to Abraham and Sarai's name to Sarah. But that wasn't the only thing that was about to change. God was about to perform a miracle by the name of Isaac. Sarah, He announced, was going to have a baby.

> I will bless her and will surely give you a son by her. I will bless her so that she will be the mother of nations; kings of peoples will come from her. (verse 16)

Can you imagine what Abraham must have thought? *God, are You kidding? I am ninety-nine years old. My wife is eighty-nine. Her womb is as good as dead. I'm a shriveled-up old man. I know You mean well, but really? A child? From Sarah?*

A short time later, the Lord appeared to Abraham with angels in the guise of three men, and he said, "I will surely return to you about this time next year, and Sarah your wife will have a son" (18:10). This time, the eavesdropping Sarah laughed. The Lord questioned the reason for her laughter and said, "Is anything too hard for the LORD?" (verse 14).

When God appeared to Abraham and introduced the name El Shaddai, God Almighty, Abraham believed that God was able to accomplish all He had promised. God's words nourished Abraham's faith that the Almighty would do what He said He would do. It didn't matter that Abraham was ninety-nine years old. It didn't matter that Sarah was eighty-nine years old. The laws of nature do not apply to the One who created them. With God, all things are possible. With the revelation of His name, God let Abraham know that His power was all sufficient and He could do anything He pleased. He was not bound by the realm of the physical world or fettered by the decisions of man. Nothing—not even a dried-up womb or a withered-up man—could stop His word from coming to pass.

So what about you? What about your situation? I ask the same question the Lord asked Sarah. "Is anything too hard for the LORD?" (Genesis 18:14).

No matter what you're going through today, you can cling to the truth that God is El Shaddai, the All-Sufficient One. He has within Himself the life-giving sustenance you need...the life-giving sustenance your heart longs for.

I encourage you to nuzzle up to El Shaddai and allow Him to calm your fears, soothe your hunger, and nourish your soul.

Let's Pray

Oh, El Shaddai, nothing is too hard for You. You have everything I need. Forgive me when I root about this earth looking for people, possessions, and power to satisfy my deepest longings. You, only You, can truly satisfy my deepest desires. You are El Shaddai, the nourisher, sustainer, and soother of my soul. In Jesus's name, amen.

Day 5

The Jealous God
El Kannah

Mary Southerland

Today's Truth

Do not worship any other god, for the LORD, whose name is Jealous, is a jealous God. (Exodus 34:14)

Friend to Friend

Shakespeare described jealousy as "the green-ey'd monster."[8] Mark Twain called it "a trade-mark of small minds."[9] I once heard it described as "the gangrene of the soul." Not a lovely picture, is it? In fact, in human terms, jealousy is usually thought of as a negative trait we need to carefully guard against. So the idea of our God as jealous can be confusing unless you think of it as Francis Thompson did.

Francis Thompson was a nineteenth-century poet, an opium addict whose sense of the divine pursuit of his soul is famously captured in his poem "The Hound of Heaven." Here is a brief excerpt:

Adown titanic glooms of chasméd fears,
    From those strong feet that followed, followed after.
        But with unhurrying chase,
        And unperturbéd pace,

Deliberate speed, majestic instancy,
They beat—and a voice beat
More instant than the feet—"
"All things betray thee, who betrayest Me."[10]

Francis describes his personal wrestling match with a jealous God who refuses to give up on what some people would describe as a loser. He was, after all, a drug addict and a fairly messed-up individual. Yet God seemed determined to love Francis no matter what the poet did or didn't do. God wanted Francis to experience His love and return it with the same intensity as it was given. Francis's poem vividly describes his attempt to escape the insistent love of God in a somewhat startling description of God as the "Hound of Heaven." Hounds are known for their tenacious and shrewd pursuit of their prey. However, their motive for capturing their prey is totally opposite to the motive of God, who pursues us like a passionate lover who will not give up until that love is returned.

Our God is a jealous God, El Kannah. The root idea in the Old Testament word *jealous* is "to become intensely red" and refers to how rising emotion colors our faces when something or someone very dear to us is threatened. Been there? I have! In fact, both the Old and New Testament words for *jealousy* are also translated "zeal." In other words, being jealous and being zealous are basically the same in the Bible. God is zealous, eager about protecting what is precious to Him. Such jealousy compels God to pursue each one of us relentlessly, no matter how we try to evade Him with our indifferent attitude or our propensity for sin. The jealousy of God is comparable to the jealous, protective passion of a parent for a child. As a mother, I know what that kind of love is like.

When our son was only six weeks old, he developed a potentially serious medical condition. When the doctor told us to immediately bring Jered to the hospital for tests, I panicked. Dan rushed home from work, and we raced to the hospital, where we were met by caring nurses and our wonderful pediatrician. After an extensive exam, the doctor said, "Okay. Let's get an IV in this little man and get him upstairs for x-rays." Seeing the look on my face, Dr. Schultz wrapped his arm around my shoulders and said, "He is going to be fine. We will take good care of him." Words of comfort, but they were not nearly enough to assuage my anguish as I pictured needles being thrust into my precious baby. And he couldn't eat in case they had to do surgery! Jered was all about eating. After his regular feeding time came and went, he screamed for food until he was hoarse. I cried along with him because I knew he was hungry, but I couldn't feed him or make him understand *why* I couldn't feed him.

The nurses, who were obviously accustomed to dealing with almost-hysterical mothers like me, reassured me repeatedly that everything was going to be fine. I wanted proof! This was not just any baby they were dealing with. Jered was *my* baby! I fully expected the claws to pop out of the ends of my fingers at any moment because, for the first time in my life, I understood what a momma bear must feel like when her cub is threatened.

The nurse assigned to insert Jered's IV was wonderful. I held him tightly as she expertly inserted the needle and quickly secured it with surgical tape. She then took a Styrofoam cup, cut it in half, and taped it over the needle so Jered couldn't accidently kick it out. And let me tell you, he was indeed kicking at that point!

The nurse then left the room so I could rock my baby and try to calm him down. Just as he drifted off to sleep, the door banged open. An x-ray technician wheeled a gurney into the room and sharply ordered, "Let's go!" He had no idea who he was dealing with.

My husband did and quickly took charge, escorting the technician into the hallway. "We will carry Jered up to the x-ray floor and will be glad to follow you," he told the man, "but we will not need that gurney until we get there." The technician started to argue but evidently reconsidered when his eyes found mine and he caught my death glare. "Fine," he said. He grabbed the IV pole and told us to follow him.

When we reached the x-ray unit, Dan gently pried Jered out of my arms and laid him on the gurney. The technician said, "We are really backed up today so let's make this quick!" He then jerked the gurney and the IV pole in opposite directions, yanking out the carefully inserted and securely taped IV. Blood spurted out of my son's leg, and he began to scream.

I don't exactly remember what happened next, but Dan does. He says I scooped Jered up in my arms and stomped my foot so loudly that nurses came running as I growled at the offending young man. I guess the technician had reached his patience limit too, because he glared back at me and said, "Lady, do you need to leave this unit?" Dan began calculating how he was going to raise my bail money when, out of the corner of his eye, he saw me approach the doomed technician, plant my finger in his chest, and whisper through clenched teeth, "Listen carefully to me, young man. I know you have a job to do, but you need to understand something right now! This is *my* baby! I am *not* going anywhere! And *you* need to watch how you treat him!" The young man quickly apologized—as did I…sort of…but I meant every word I had spoken. Fortunately, the x-rays confirmed that Jered did not need to have surgery. Afterward, he gulped down two full bottles in record time, and I let the technician live—and we headed home instead of to jail. I was and still am a jealous parent, passionate and zealous about my children.

Don't doubt for a minute that God is jealous for you, girlfriend. He is standing right beside you, wrapping His arms of love around your wounded heart. Listen closely as He declares that you are His child. You belong to Him and He is not going anywhere! He is El Kannah, forever with you and pursuing you with all His love-filled heart.

Let's Pray

Father God, I am just flat-out amazed by the way You love me. To think that You are jealous for me rocks my world! I know me…and I simply cannot comprehend why You love me so much. But, God, by sheer faith, I thank You and praise You for loving me and pursuing me—even when I don't want to be found. Thank You for never letting me go. Help me to love You more and to share that love with others. In Jesus's name, amen.

Now It's Your Turn

Time for Reflection

- God is Elohim, our Creator. On Day 1, Sharon stated that knowing God as Elohim answers three big questions for all of us: Who am I? Where did I come from? Why am I here? Scripture tells us that humanity was separated from all other creation in that we were created in God's image. What do you think it means to be created in the image of God?
- Read Genesis 1:31: "And God saw everything that he had made, and behold, it was very good. And there was evening and there was morning, the sixth day" (ESV).

  How did God feel about what He had made?
- Based upon God's response to His creation, what conclusion can you draw about your value as a woman created in the image of God?
- Does knowing you are created to reflect God (to glorify God) affect how you live? Is there any change you need to make to better reflect Him?
- On Day 2 we came face to face with El Olam, the Everlasting God, who was and is and is to come. Our problems are finite; they have a beginning and an end. God's ability to meet us at each challenge is not limited by space or time. Are there people or challenges you need to entrust to God's eternal purposes and everlasting strength? Discuss.

- Though we face temporal hardships, the Bible instructs believers to walk by faith, not by sight (2 Corinthians 5:7). What would it look like if you chose to walk by faith in the everlasting God and not by sight this week? Be specific.
- Another name of God is Yahweh Tsuri: God My Rock. In the Old Testament, rocks were used for many purposes, such as for building walls or memorials and for shade and protection. Read 1 Samuel 7:12: "Then Samuel took a stone and set it up between Mizpah and Shen and called its name Ebenezer; for he said, 'Till now the LORD has helped us'" (ESV).

  Samuel used a stone to remind him of the strong deliverance of God. What ways do you remember and celebrate your steadfast, faithful God?
- Read and meditate on Isaiah 26:3–4: "You will keep in perfect peace him whose mind is steadfast, because he trusts in you. Trust in the LORD forever, for the LORD, the LORD, is the Rock eternal."

  Describe a time when God was your Rock or when you have felt held in perfect peace by Him. What did that look like and feel like?

  ____

  ____

  ____
- El Shaddai, our All-Sufficient One, is faithful and loving to sustain and nourish His people. Can you think of a time God sustained you? Nourished you? If you are doing this study in a group, share your experience. If you're doing this study alone, record it here as a praise offering to God.

  ____

  ____

Consider your life. What or whom have you looked to for sustenance or satisfaction other than God? Did it satisfy in the long run? What changes do you need to make in your current life to be sure you're trusting God alone to meet your needs?

Look up 2 Corinthians 9:8 and Ephesians 3:20–21, which speak to God's ability and willingness to satisfy our longings. Then fill in the blanks below.

"And God is ________ to make all __________ abound to you, so that in ______ ____________ at ______ __________, having ______ that you ________, you ________ ____________ in every good work." (2 Corinthians 9:8)

"Now to him who ____ ________ to do immeasurably ________ than _______ we _______ or ______________, according to his __________ that is at work ____________ _______, to him be glory in the church and in Christ Jesus throughout all generations, for ever and ever! Amen." (Ephesians 3:20–21)

Summarize the message of these verses.

____

____

What is God saying to you at this time about your seemingly impossible situation?

God's jealousy is one of His holy attributes and applies to many areas of our lives as well as to the nature of God Himself. He is El Kannah, the Jealous God. We don't have to read very far in the Bible before we hear God saying, "You shall not make for yourself an idol, or any likeness of what is in heaven above or on the earth beneath or in the water under the earth. You shall not worship them or serve them; for I, the LORD your God, am a jealous God" (Exodus 20:4–5, NASB). Read the following verses and fill in the blanks.

"For the LORD has chosen Jacob to be his own, Israel to be his treasured possession." (Psalm 135:4)

God is jealous for the nation of ____________.

"I am the LORD; that is my name! I will not give my glory to another or my praise to idols." (Isaiah 42:8)

God is jealous for His _________.

"For I [Paul] am jealous for you with a godly jealousy; for I betrothed you to one husband, so that to Christ I might present you as a pure virgin." (2 Corinthians 11:2, NASB)

God is jealous for ____________________

How do you suppose this translates to the priorities God wants you to set when it comes to the people and things in your life?

- Do you feel it is important for you to pay attention to the jealousy of God? Why or why not?
- Wrap up your response time with prayer. Move from confession, to adoration, to thanksgiving, and end with your petitions (personal prayer needs).

Going Deeper with God

List: the names of God and their meanings that were covered in the devotions this week.

1. ________________________________
2. ________________________________
3. ________________________________
4. ________________________________
5. ________________________________

Read: Genesis 1 and 2.

Contemplate: In Genesis 1 and 2, you'll notice that the writer repeats the creation account. The second account focuses on the creation of man. What do you learn about Elohim from these two chapters? How have you witnessed God as Elohim in your life?

Your GiG *Knowing God by Name* Journal

Spend a few moments contemplating and journaling about some of the scriptural truths that moved your heart as you read the devotions this week. Then use the space below to collect your thoughts or write a prayer of response to God.

The eternal God is your refuge, and his everlasting arms are under you. (Deuteronomy 33:27, NLT*)*

Day 1

I Am, the Self-Existent One

Yahweh

Sharon Jaynes

Today's Truth

God said to Moses, "I AM WHO I AM. This is what you are to say to the Israelites: 'I AM has sent me to you.'… Say to the Israelites, 'The LORD [Yahweh], the God of your fathers—the God of Abraham, the God of Isaac and the God of Jacob—has sent me to you.' This is my name forever, the name by which I am to be remembered from generation to generation." (Exodus 3:14–15)

Friend to Friend

What do you need today? No matter your answer, I have some great news. Whatever you need, God is.

When we open the book of Exodus, we find God's chosen people in bondage, slaves to the Egyptian powerhouse. After settling in Egypt during the time of Joseph, the Israelites had become so numerous that the pharaoh made them slaves in order to subdue them. However, hard labor and difficult circumstances didn't destroy them; the challenges only made them stronger (a truth for all of us to hang on to, but a story for another day). So the pharaoh came up with another idea: "Every [Hebrew] boy that is born you must throw into the Nile, but let every girl live" (Exodus 1:22).

When Moses was born, his mother followed Pharaoh's command, but not before placing him in his own personal ark and setting him afloat. Pharaoh's daughter rescued Moses from the river and raised him as her own son. Forty years later, Moses was disturbed about the fate of his people. He came upon an Egyptian beating a Hebrew, murdered the Egyptian, and hid him in the sand. When Pharaoh heard of this, he sought to kill Moses. In one day, Moses went from being a prince of Egypt to a felon on the run.

In Exodus 3, we find Moses taking care of sheep on the far side of the Midian desert. While taking care of the flock, he noticed a bush was burning without being burned up. When God saw that Moses had "gone over to look," He called to him, "Moses! Moses!"

> And Moses said, "Here I am."
>
> "Do not come any closer," God said. "Take off your sandals, for the place where you are standing is holy ground." Then he said, "I am the God of your father, the God of Abraham, the God of Isaac and the God of Jacob." At this, Moses hid his face, because he was afraid to look at God.
>
> The LORD said, "I have indeed *seen* the misery of my people in Egypt. I have *heard* them crying out because of their slave drivers, and I am *concerned* about their suffering. So I have come down to rescue them from the hand of the Egyptians and to bring them up out of that land into a good and spacious land, a land flowing with milk and honey." (verses 4–8)

God told Moses of His plan to free the Hebrew nation from Egyptian slavery. That was great news! Then God said, "and I am sending you" to do it (verse 10). That was not great news…at least, not to Moses. He argued with God, telling Him all the reasons He had the wrong man for the job. "Who am I, that I should go to Pharaoh and bring the Israelites out of Egypt?" And God answered, "I will be with you" (verses 11–12).

But Moses continued to argue.

> "Suppose I go to the Israelites and say to them, 'The God of your fathers has sent me to you,' and they ask me, 'What is his name?' Then what shall I tell them?"
>
> God said to Moses, "I AM WHO I AM. This is what you are to say to the Israelites: 'I AM has sent me to you.'"
>
> God also said to Moses, "Say to the Israelites, 'The LORD [Yahweh], the God of your fathers—the God of Abraham, the God of Isaac and the God of Jacob—has sent me to you.' This is my name forever, the name by which I am to be remembered from generation to generation." (verses 13–15)

I AM. He was. He is. He always has been and always will be. He is the Self-Existent One with no beginning and no end.

God uses two forms of the same name in this passage. I AM is the first-person form of the verb *to be* and is the name He uses when speaking of Himself. LORD, or Yahweh in the Hebrew, is the third-person form of the same verb translated "He is." When God speaks of Himself, He says, "I AM," and when we speak of Him, we say, "He is."

Originally, the Name was only four letters: YHWH. Later,

scribes inserted vowels to form the word *Yahweh.* Some Bible translations render the same name as Jehovah. YHWH appears in the Old Testament more than 6,800 times, and is found in every book except Esther, Ecclesiastes, and Song of Songs. When you see the name rendered *LORD* (using all capitals) in the Bible, it is referring to Yahweh. When you see the word *Lord* (with lowercase letters), it is referring to a different name: Adonai. (Gwen will talk about that in the next chapter.)

The name YHWH was considered so holy to the early rabbinical scribes, they wouldn't even write the letters. They used "the Name," "the Unutterable Name," "the Great and Terrible Name," or "the Holy Name" whenever it appeared.

As I mentioned in the introduction, I visited an exhibit of the Dead Sea Scrolls when they came to my hometown. Over 230 biblical texts, representing nearly every book of the Old Testament, have been discovered in those desert caves so far. When I compared the various Hebrew parchments to the English translations posted below them, I noticed four dots where the name YHWH should have been. The scribes revered the name YHWH so much they wouldn't even write it.

You can imagine the Pharisees' surprise when Jesus said, "I tell you the truth, before Abraham was even born, I AM!" (John 8:58, NLT).

Jesus echoed God's words of Exodus 3:14 and, in those two little words, expressed the eternity of His being and His oneness with the Father. Jesus, who is the exact representation of God's character and His ways (John 14:8–9; Hebrews 1:3), went on to make seven other "I am" statements. He is the bread of life who sustains you (John 6:35), the light of the world who guides you (John 8:12), the gate who opens heaven for you (John 10:9), the good shepherd who cares for you (John 10:11–14), the resurrection and the life who gave His life for you (John 11:25), the way, the truth, and the life who offers abundant life on earth and eternal life hereafter to you (John 14:6), and the vine who supplies your every need (John 15:1, 5).

Did you notice that God called Moses by name? Oh, sister, God knows your name. God calls your name. Just as He had *seen* the affliction of the Israelites, *heard* the cries of His people, and was *concerned* about their suffering, I AM sees you, hears you, and is *concerned* about your suffering.

I AM. What a name. Whatever you need...God is.

Today, know that you can run to the great I AM in every circumstance of life. He holds the keys to unlock every difficult situation. He is the bread to satisfy every hunger, the living water to quench every thirst, and the light to illumine every dark path. He is never stymied by your past, surprised by your present, or worried about your future. HE IS.

I pray that you will turn aside as Moses did and notice the great I AM right smack-dab in the middle of your busy day.

Let's Pray

Dear Lord, I praise Your holy name. You are the great I AM. You have no beginning and You'll have no end. And yet, in all Your greatness, You call me by name. I echo Moses's words today: "Here I am." In Jesus's name, amen.

Lord and Master
Adonai

Gwen Smith

Today's Truth

Tremble, O earth, at the presence of the Lord, at the presence of the God of Jacob. (Psalm 114:7)

Friend to Friend

Have you ever been undone before the Lord? Have you shaken your head in awe at the mere thought of being accepted as holy in His sight? The prophet Isaiah experienced God in His splendor, through a vision that left him flat-out speechless.

> In the year that King Uzziah died, I saw the Lord seated on a throne, high and exalted, and the train of his robe filled the temple. Above him were seraphs, each with six wings: With two wings they covered their faces, with two they covered their feet, and with two they were flying. And they were calling to one another:
>
> "Holy, holy, holy is the Lord Almighty;
> the whole earth is full of His glory."

> At the sound of their voices the doorposts and thresholds shook and the temple was filled with smoke.
>
> "Woe to me!" I cried. "I am ruined! For I am a man of unclean lips, and I live among a people of unclean lips, and my eyes have seen the King, the LORD Almighty." (Isaiah 6:1–5)

I shudder to think how often I approach this awesome, powerful, holy God without the reverence that is due Him. I confess that every fiber of my being should fall before Him and shout "I am undone!" so much more than I actually do. Isaiah's response takes us to the place we should be: face down before our holy, royal, heavenly King, our worthy Master, our Adonai.

As a worship leader, I often find myself feeling unworthy of my calling to lead people into God's holy presence. The fact of the matter is, I am unworthy of the call. I'm a holy mess who couldn't begin to measure up to God's standard of perfection if I tried. Like the apostle Paul writing in Romans 7:15, I find that I continually do what I don't want to do and don't do what I want to do! My bent is selfishness; I constantly bow to my own will instead of to the will of God. At times I explode like a geyser and allow anger to get the better of me. I can be stubborn and—honestly, the list of my shortcomings could go on and on. But God, through His only Son, Jesus Christ, made a way for me to be holy and acceptable in His sight.

How amazing is that?

How amazing is His love?

He made a way for each of us to be forgiven! When we place our faith in Jesus Christ, confess our sins, and ask to be forgiven, the Bible tells us that God forgives our sins (1 John 1:9). Not only does God forgive our sins, but He also sees us as holy because of Jesus.

Holy! Can you imagine? You and me? Oh, friend, we have so much to be thankful for!

Since this is true and because God's forgiveness is life changing, the Bible instructs us not to be enslaved to our fallen natures. "For sin shall not be your master, because you are not under law, but under grace" (Romans 6:14). As women of grace, our master is to be none other than the righteousness of Christ: Adonai.

Adonai is a Hebrew name for God meaning "master, ruler, owner, lord."[11] It is the generic term for *lord* in Hebrew. It is first seen in Scripture when Abram, longing for an heir, cries out to God in Genesis 15:2, "O Lord God, what will you give me, for I continue childless, and the heir of my house is Eliezer of Damascus?" (ESV). Abraham called out to God as his Master. He looked to Him in prayer through confusing circumstances. He connected his hopes to Adonai and revered Him as the One who held the answers to life in His hands. You and I should do the same. When we accept God as Master—sovereign over all—then He becomes greater and we become less.

When we get to know God as our Adonai, we will be more inclined to seek Him and revere Him in appropriate measures to His glory. A few years back, as I considered the weight of this—and meditated on the experience of the prophet Isaiah in falling before God in awe of His presence—I was inspired to write a worship song called "Holy Adonai." I'd love to share it with you.

Holy Adonai

Words and music by Gwen Smith[12]

Majesty
Mighty King

You are God
Everything
Holy One
Father, Son
Matchless Lord
We're undone

You are the One deserving praise
You are the Lord of all my days
You are the royal King of kings
The only reason we can sing
You rule in splendor from Your throne
Within Your grace our hope is known
You are the God who reigns on high
Holy Adonai

You are holy, holy
You are holy, holy
You are worthy, worthy
You are worthy, worthy
Worthy, worthy

Girlfriend, I can't help but join the heavenly creatures as I shout from my home in North Carolina to you across the globe: "Holy, holy, holy is the LORD Almighty; the whole earth is full of his glory" (Isaiah 6:3)! As you read this devotion in Maine, Florida, Pennsylvania, Texas, Idaho, California, New York, Indiana, Brazil, Guatemala, Germany, India, Uganda, Croatia, Australia, China, or Norway—in whatever city, whatever state, whatever country you reside—would you join heaven's song and lift the name of the Lord high today as a united body of sisters? Let us be undone together and bow our hearts before Adonai, our Lord and Master, with a renewed awe of His greatness.

He is worthy!

Let's Pray

Most holy Lord, Adonai, I pray that You would forgive me for all the times I have come into Your presence lacking reverence. You are worthy of all praise! May You become greater in my life and may I become less. Empower me to live a life that points to Your glorious splendor. Thank You, Lord! In Jesus's name, amen.

The Ancient of Days
Atik Yomin

Sharon Jaynes

Today's Truth

I kept looking until thrones were set up, and the Ancient of Days took His seat; His vesture was like white snow and the hair of His head like pure wool. (Daniel 7:9, NASB)

Friend to Friend

Hiphuggers. Bell-bottoms. Tie-dyed T-shirts. Platform shoes. Guitars. Loud music. "Pass It On." Bibles. Teenagers. Long stringy hair parted down the middle on both boys and girls. Put all that together and you have a snapshot of some of the best days of my teen years.

I became a Christian when I was fourteen, during the Jesus Movement of the seventies, and Jesus moved right into my heart to stay. My parents were not Christians at the time, and ours was not a happy family. Our home teemed with tension and vacillated between violent bouts of fighting and passive-aggressive weeks of silence.

Soon after my decision to follow Jesus, a group of businessmen in my community had a vision to open a Christian coffeehouse. Their dream was to provide a safe place for teens to congregate and grow in their faith. Their hope was to bring in college-aged Bible teachers on weeknights and contemporary Christian bands on weekends.

God was all in favor of blessing our merry band of Jesus-lovin', hormone-powered, tie-dyed teens, and provided the perfect venue for the dream to materialize. Right in the middle of our sleepy little downtown, tucked in a side-street alcove, sat an abandoned bar that had been shut down for selling alcohol to minors. The name of the bar? The Ancient of Days. Sometimes God is so outlandishly obvious you just have to laugh. The businessmen bought the building and kept the name. Talk about redemption! What the devil meant for evil, God clearly meant for good (Genesis 50:20).

At fifteen, I wasn't sure what the Ancient of Days actually meant, but this cubbyhole tucked between a ladies' dress shop and a photography studio became my refuge in an uncertain world. Now, as an adult, I soak in the name, steep in the name, marinate in the name. God is my Ancient of Days who always has been and always will be watching over my life—and watching over yours. "Long before he laid down earth's foundations, he had us in mind, had settled on us as the focus of his love, to be made whole and holy by his love" (Ephesians 1:4, MSG).

Among all the authors of the Bible, only Daniel used the name Ancient of Days in describing God. The prophet had a vision of four world empires that rose to great power and prominence, only to fall and crumble into insignificance. When a fifth world power emerged in the vision, a power that many theologians believe represents the Antichrist of the end times, the Ancient of Days took His seat on the throne.

As I looked,
thrones were set in place,

and the *Ancient of Days* took his seat.
His clothing was as white as snow;
the hair of his head was white like wool.
His throne was flaming with fire,
and its wheels were all ablaze.
A river of fire was flowing,
coming out from before him.
Thousands upon thousands attended him;
ten thousand times ten thousand stood before him.
The court was seated,
and the books were opened. (Daniel 7:9–10)

The Ancient of Days destroyed the Antichrist and opened heaven's gate for Christ's return. "He [Jesus] approached the Ancient of Days and was led into his presence. He was given authority, glory and sovereign power; all peoples, nations and men of every language worshiped him. His dominion is an everlasting dominion that will not pass away, and his kingdom is one that will never be destroyed" (verses 13–14).

The name Ancient of Days, Atik Yomin in Aramaic[13], does not point to an elderly ruler made feeble by age, but to a divine ruler who is eternally all powerful. He is the everlasting God who rules in sovereignty. The name Ancient of Days points to God as the divine Judge. That is good news for those who have accepted Jesus as Lord and Savior, because "there is now no condemnation for those who are in Christ Jesus" (Romans 8:1). However, it is bad news for those who have refused to bend the knee and submit to the lordship of Christ—for those who have not believed on Jesus as Lord and Savior (Romans 10:9–13).

How wonderful that we, God's children, don't have to fear the coming judgment. "The Ancient of Days came and pronounced judgment in favor of the saints of the Most High, and the time came when they possessed the kingdom" (Daniel 7:22). (In the New Testament, Christians are referred to as saints. The word means "set apart.")

I encourage you to go back and read all of Daniel's vision recorded in chapter 7. It is mysteriously weighty. No wonder Daniel said his face turned pale and he kept the matter to himself (verse 28).

And while I will never totally understand all that the vision means, I can grab hold of the name the Ancient of Days with both hands. God always has been and always will be. He had no predecessor and He'll have no successor. You can't impeach Him, and He's not going to resign. He had no beginning, and He'll have no end. He simply *is.* While everything around us changes, the Ancient of Days remains the same.

I'm reminded of the words to the old hymn by Walter Chalmers Smith:

> Immortal, invisible, God only wise,
> In light inaccessible hid from our eyes,
> Most blessed, most glorious, the Ancient of Days,
> Almighty, victorious, Thy great Name we praise.

The Ancient of Days—an old bar turned sanctuary—provided a safe haven during my tumultuous childhood. The Ancient of Days—an unchanging God who defies time—offers a safe haven for all my tomorrows.

Whatever you are going through today, know this: God is on His throne. He's in control. I am not on the throne. The president is not on the throne. World powers are not on the throne.

The Ancient of Days sits on the throne. His rule is right and His reign is sure.

"How great you are, O Sovereign LORD! There is no one like you, and there is no God but you, as we have heard with our own ears" (2 Samuel 7:22). Most blessed, most glorious, the Ancient of Days, almighty, victorious, Thy great name we praise.

Let's Pray

I praise You, Ancient of Days. When my life is changing too quickly and too often, I rest in knowing that You never change. You are the Ancient of Days who sits on the throne. You had no beginning and will have no end. Your rule is right and Your reign is sure. In Jesus's name, amen.

The Most High God

El Elyon

Gwen Smith

Today's Truth

They remembered that God was their Rock, that God Most High was their Redeemer. (Psalm 78:35)

Friend to Friend

My heart plays Ping-Pong. It shifts focus from one affection to another faster than you can say, "Squirrel!" I have never been diagnosed with ADD or ADHD—or any other condition with scary capital letters—but I've surely been known to major on some minors in my day. Practically every day. I worry about things that don't really matter, at least not eternally.

In the wee hours of one particular day, I poured some hot coffee, grabbed my prayer journal and my Bible, and headed to the couch to spend time with God. My heart spilled with worship as I fixed my affections on Him. Fueled and focused, I was prepared to start my day.

Awhile later, my son came downstairs ready for school. We exchanged tender morning greetings and hugs before he grabbed a bowl for cereal. But when he sat down to eat, I realized he was wearing two different socks. As he ate his breakfast, I tried to lovingly influence him toward a matching pair—to no avail. *Humph!* When he left for the bus stop, I lamented. *Where have I gone wrong with this child? Why does his thirteen-year-old brain not realize it is inappropriate to wear mismatched socks? What will people think? Surely the teachers will have a juicy gossip session in the lunchroom about how awful and inadequate I am as a mother because my "it's all good" child went to school with two different socks!*

AS IF it matters.

Ping. Pong.

My heart can turn on a dime. One moment it is fixed on the Lord, and the next it is prioritized on drama. Does God care if my son's socks match? I'm thinking, *No.* Is it okay to want my children to wear matching socks? Yes. Surely I can speak into a practical matter, but the *way* I respond matters more, especially if things don't go my way. *Let it go, already.*

I really do need to let it go.

I need to let a lot of things go. I need to let go of reactions, emotions, activities, or thoughts that don't honor God. He wants to be our top priority! That's why we were created. To love Him above all things. He wants the details, activities, and decisions of our lives to be prioritized around Him—not just our Sunday mornings and major decisions but our *every* morning and our *every* decision. We must look to Him as our desire, our ultimate, our obsession. When we do so, the rest of life falls into place.

The appropriateness of maintaining our focus on God is indicated in the name El Elyon. This Hebrew term for God can be translated two ways: "the Most High God" or "God Most High." Either way, they mean the same thing: He is to be preeminent in our lives. He is supreme. There is nothing above Him or beyond Him.

In her book *Obsessed,* author and speaker Hayley DiMarco said it this way: "If you claim two obsessions, then you are not truly obsessed with both. No one is obsessed part-time."[14]

As we saw last week through the name El Kannah, God is jealous for us. He wants us to be obsessed with Him and Him alone. "You shall tear down their altars and break their pillars and cut down their Asherim (for you shall worship no other god, for the LORD, whose name is Jealous, is a jealous God)" (Exodus 34:13–14, ESV). In other words, "Get rid of your idols, people. Walk away from anything in your life that takes precedence over Me!"

We honor God as El Elyon when our affections for Him and His ways are prioritized above all else. The Lord wants us to be focused worshipers. To have hearts that look to Him and His strength, seeking His face always (Psalm 105:4). When we interact with our Father as God Most High, we fully entrust our plans, our desires, our families, our careers, our lives, our everything to His will alone. As the psalmist wrote, "I cry out to God Most High, to God, who fulfills his purpose for me" (Psalm 57:2).

I'm so encouraged by what Scripture says here: when I cry out to God and make Him my ultimate, He fulfills His purpose for me. *Yes, please!* That's what I want. His purpose, not mine. More of Him, less of me. You see, we don't have to try to find our happiness and purpose in other things. When we give priority to God Most High in our lives, He fulfills us in a way that none of these other things can!

A. W. Tozer wrote, "What comes into our minds when we think about God is the most important thing about us."[15] He also listed off these telling "Rules for Self Discovery":

1. What we want most
2. What we think about most
3. How we use our money

4. What we do with our leisure time
5. The company we enjoy
6. Who and what we admire
7. What we laugh at[16]

Tozer summed it up beautifully. Every aspect of our lives should reveal the precedence we give to our Most High God.

What does this mean in your life, practically speaking? What does El Elyon mean to your worries and fears? When you measure the concerns of your life against El Elyon, the pinnacle of existence, do they still look so big? What does El Elyon mean to your busy life, your weight-loss goals, or your relationships? What dominates your thoughts? Are you more concerned about pleasing man or pleasing God?

This is where the self meets the Supreme—and you decide who to serve.

Where your *ping* meets your *pong*.

You must choose what, or who, will be Most High in your life.

The psalmist chose what is best as he sang to El Elyon, "I will give thanks to the LORD with my whole heart; I will recount all of your wonderful deeds. I will be glad and exult in you; I will sing praise to your name, O Most High" (Psalm 9:1–2, ESV).

Will you revere God as El Elyon today?

Let's Pray

Dear Lord, El Elyon, I really want to get this one! Help me to place You above all and before all. Show me what that looks like in the midst of my drama. Help me to yield to You when I want to take control. Be my everything. In Jesus's name, amen.

The King of Kings

Basileus Basileōn

Gwen Smith

Today's Truth

God, the blessed and only Ruler, the King of kings and Lord of lords, who alone is immortal and who lives in unapproachable light, whom no one has seen or can see. To him be honor and might forever. Amen. (1 Timothy 6:15–16)

Friend to Friend

It was shockingly early when the alarm clock invaded my dreams, screaming at me to wake up. Even the sun was still sleeping as I rose. With heavy eyelids and a groggy mind, I forced myself to crawl out from the cuddly warmth of my bed and venture downstairs.

The kids had set their alarm clocks as well. We trickled down, one sleepy Smith at a time, and met in our jammies for the big event. It was April 29, 2011. Prince William and Catherine Middleton were about to be married, and we were giddy-excited to watch the event live from the cozy comfort of our living room couch.

It was worth the early wake-up just to see the hats that the women were wearing. Major wow! They were so elaborate! Some were even a bit crazy. As the wedding guests filed into the church, the kids and I chatted nonstop about the dresses the women wore, the celestial music echoing throughout the cathedral, and the ornate beauty of Westminster Abbey.

As Kate made her way toward her groom, my eyes leaked joy. There's just something undeniably special about a bride's walk down the aisle that messes with my makeup. The ceremony was magic. Brimming with Scripture and promise. Meaningful vows were exchanged, and before we knew it, the bride and groom were married.

Regal smiles lit up our living room when the Duke and Duchess of Cambridge emerged as husband and wife and made their way to Buckingham Palace for the royal reception hosted by Her Majesty, the Queen of England. They waved jubilantly to the thousands upon thousands of well-wishers along the road as the world celebrated with them.

We have such a fascination with royalty! We love the regal bells and whistles with all of the fairy tale happenings. Decades before William and Kate's famed nuptials, the wedding of Prince Charles and Lady Diana Spencer held global attention. Before that, the world was smitten with the storybook romance and marriage between American actress Grace Kelly and Prince Rainier III of Monaco.

Yet, for all the fanfare that royal families bring to society, many reigning monarchs wield little political power. Most earthly kings and queens don't establish laws or truly rule the people as royalty once did. Even so, these families do influence the culture, but God is the King of kings.

The Greek term for "King of kings" is *basileus basileōn.*[17] "The name *King of kings* denotes sovereignty and authority; the name *Lord of lords* signifies majesty and power. Every ruler, all nations, and all people are subject to him; and anyone belonging to either the angelic world or humanity who determines to fight him faces a losing battle and utter ruin."[18]

God is a not like earthly kings. He's got game! He is a King *with* power. He is the King of kings! Supreme in authority, He rules from a heavenly throne that is illuminated by His glory. When we recognize Him as King of kings, God is positioned in our hearts as the supreme ruler, as the absolute authority, as the powerful Lord for whom we are desperate. His reign is eternal and supreme, yet His reign is intimately personal.

Our holy God is not some distant, unfeeling ruler who pats us on the head and graciously allows us to be His humble servants. He is a caring King who loves each of His subjects beyond understanding. Believe me, this flesh-and-blood testimony comes from a woman who knows what it's like to be tangled in the knots of sin and shame. From a woman who knows the freedom of forgiveness—a woman who delights to revere her all-compassionate King of mercy. I'm not who I once was, all because my Savior, the King of kings, wore a thorny crown and conquered death. Now that's power, friend!

I am a woman who now confidently approaches the throne of grace because of the finished work done by Jesus Christ (Hebrews 4:16). The God of grace is personal, and you'd better believe He's powerful. Scripture is filled with rich praise for our King of kings:

> The LORD has established his throne in heaven, and his kingdom rules over all. (Psalm 103:19)

> No one is like you, O LORD; you are great, and your name is mighty in power. Who should not revere you, O King of the

> nations? This is your due.... The Lord is the true God; he is the living God, the eternal King. (Jeremiah 10:6–7, 10)

> How awesome is the Lord Most High, the great King over all the earth! (Psalm 47:2)

> But you, O Lord, sit enthroned forever; your renown endures through all generations. (Psalm 102:12)

Have you experienced the power of the King of kings in your life? Do you know the freedom of forgiveness? God loved you so much that He made a way for you to have a fresh start in life through Jesus: a fresh start, a clean heart, and a royal inheritance. That, my friend, should make us all leak with joy!

> Now to the King eternal, immortal, invisible, the only God, be honor and glory for ever and ever. Amen. (1 Timothy 1:17)

Let's Pray

Holy God, King of kings, You are more glorious and powerful than I can possibly imagine! Thank You for crowning me with grace through Jesus Christ. Thank You that Your grace is enough to free me from anything or anyone that attempts to reign over my life. All glory and honor be to You, Lord! In Jesus's name, amen.

Now It's Your Turn

Time for Reflection

- In the book of Exodus, God told Moses that He is I AM WHO I AM, the Self-Existent One with no beginning and no end. He also said that He, Yahweh, was sending Moses on a mission to free His people. Moses was not happy about God's plan! He tried to convince God that He had chosen the wrong guy for the job. Describe a time in your life when you were reluctant to do something you felt God was calling you to do.
- Can you relate to Moses's fears in Exodus 3:11, 13; 4:1, 10? Go back and note God's response to each objection Moses raised.

  Moses's objection—3:11 I am nobody
  God's response—3:12 I am with you
  Moses's objection—3:13 Who sent you
  God's response—3:14 I am Who I am
  Moses's objection—4:1 ________________
  God's response—4:2–5 ________________
  Moses's objection—4:10 I don't speak well
  God's response—4:11–12 I will teach you
- Have you ever felt hesitant to follow God's direction? Discuss how God's response to Moses's objections might apply to your objections as well.
- When you think of God, what comes to your mind? Read Psalm 103:1–14 and note the picture the psalmist paints of the

Lord. Make a list of His characteristics found in these verses.

Slow to anger, patient,
compassion

- Read Philippians 4:19: "And my God will supply every need of yours according to his riches in glory in Christ Jesus" (ESV).

  What is the promise of Philippians 4:19? Eternal Life
- What need are you having difficulty trusting to I AM? Be specific.
- How would your perspective change if you allowed God to replace your fears with trust? No worries
- On a scale of 1 to 5, how willing are you to trust I AM to be that for you today?

  1 = Unwilling (Not even interested.)

  2 = Slightly willing (I'm warming up to the idea, but am not quite there yet.)

  3 = One foot in / one foot out (I trust Him sometimes, but find it hard to let go.)

  4 = Pretty willing (I trust Him, but still fret a bit.)

  5 = All in! (What needs? God's so got this one.)
- The prophet Isaiah had a humbling experience in the presence of God, where he fell face down in recognition of his own depravity in light of God's majesty. He bowed low in repentance before Adonai, his Master. Have you ever felt unworthy to approach God's throne because of sin? How does the scriptural promise of God's unconditional love and grace through Christ affect your response to His holiness?
- El Elyon, the Most High God, desires to be our holy obsession. He is preeminent. Supreme above all. List two specific ways your life would be different if you evaluated every day, every response,

I Can Only Imagine - Song

and every personal priority according to the supremacy of El Elyon.

- What should your relationship with El Elyon mean to your biggest fear, foe, or fret?
- In a world filled with flawed rulers and governmental leaders, we can rest in the sovereign power, perfection, and authority of God, our King of kings. Read 1 Peter 2:9 and fill in the blanks to learn who God says you are.

  "But you are a ______________, a ______________ ______________, a ______________ ______________, a ______________ to God…" (1 Peter 2:9a)
- Pretty impressive, right? Do you live like that's who you are? Why or why not?
- What does the rest of the verse say you are supposed to do because of who you are? Fill in the blanks.

  "…that you may ______________ the ______________ of him who called you out of darkness into his wonderful light." (1 Peter 2:9b)

  What should this look like in your life?
- Wrap up your response time with prayer. Move from confession, to adoration, to thanksgiving, and end with your petitions (personal prayer needs).

Going Deeper with God

List: the names of God and their meanings that were covered in the devotions this week.

1. ______________________________
2. ______________________________

3. ______________________________
4. ______________________________
5. ______________________________

Read: Psalm 103.

Worship: Take a few moments to hum or sing a favorite song that focuses on the awesomeness of God. (Here are some suggestions: "I Exalt Thee," "Heart of Worship," "How Great Is Our God," "How Great Thou Art," "Fairest Lord Jesus," "Doxology.")

Listen and **reflect:** Find the song "El Elyon" here at www.girlfriendsingod.com/2012/worship-el-elyon/.

Your GiG *Knowing God by Name* Journal

Spend a few moments contemplating and journaling about some of the scriptural truths that moved your heart as you read the devotions this week. Then use the space below to collect your thoughts or write a prayer of response to God.

____

____

____

____

____

____

____

____

____

3-4-16

Shari brown - foot surgery

Becky Schwintz & husband

Barbara Barnes

Jeff Prince - Carol's cousin

Benton - heart

Martha Hellums

Don Peters - cancer - Judy Nardini's friend

Brandon White - depression

Travis Todd - cancer

I cry out to God Most High, to God, who fulfills his purpose for me. (Psalm 57:2)

Day 1

All Present

Gwen Smith

Today's Truth

Fear not, for...I have summoned you by name; you are mine. When you pass through the waters, I will be with you. (Isaiah 43:1–2)

Friend to Friend

Just as we walked into the opening session of a marriage conference we'd been looking forward to, my husband's cell phone rang. He answered the call, and we took our seats. As the emcee kicked off the weekend with gracious greetings, Brad leaned over and whispered in my ear, "Preston fell on a rock at camp and is on his way to urgent care to get stitches in his chin."

Seeing the alarm on my face, he took my hand and whispered reassurance. "It's just a few stitches. He'll be okay, honey."

My stomach flip-flopped. We locked eyes in shared pain, both wounded in the heart for our firstborn son. This was *not* how we had imagined the start of our weekend away. As the session got underway, my momma-bear instincts kicked in and my mind reeled. Though he was a hundred miles away and though he's a man-cub teenager, I ached to be at Preston's side while the doctor stitched up his chin. I am *always* by his side when he gets hurt. Still, I took comfort in knowing that this was "just a few stitches."

As that first session came to a close in prayer, Brad's cell phone invaded the quiet. He leaped up and left the room to get an update on Preston. Right behind him, I asked repeatedly, "What are they saying? Is everything okay?"

"He said that Preston broke his jaw," Brad said with a tone of disbelief. Again he said, "The x-rays showed that he broke his jaw. I can't believe this. They need us to come get him and take him to Charlotte. He might need surgery."

Gripped by his words, I struggled to think clearly. *A broken jaw? Surgery? It was just supposed to be a few stitches! Well, it's probably just a small fracture. I really hate that I'm not with him right now...* Bags were quickly packed and by the time darkness fell on North Carolina, Charlotte was on the horizon.

The next several hours were a blur of doctors, x-rays, CAT scans, and surgery plans. Bad news gave way to worse as we learned that Preston didn't just break his jaw—he broke his jaw in three places, and, as the doctor phrased it: "He pretty much broke his jaw as bad as you can break a jaw." Nice.

Our son was wheeled into surgery, and the wait was on...and on...and on. The heart distance between the operating room and the waiting room was a thousand miles. It killed me not to hold Preston's hand and stroke his hair while his jaw was reconstructed for seven and a half hours.

In the wee hours of the morning, surgery was complete. Brad and I rushed to his side as they brought Preston to his room, and though he was heavily sedated, I reached for his hand and assured him, "Preston! I'm right here! I'm right by your side. I will stay here beside you. I know you're in pain, buddy, but you're going to heal well now. I'm right here and I love you."

His eyes flickered open for a split second to let Brad and me know that he heard our love. Then he drifted back to postsurgical sleep.

Several times an hour the nurses came in to check his vitals. I hadn't slept in nearly a day and was thoroughly exhausted, but each time a nurse entered the room, I sprang to his side and whispered to my wounded child, "I'm right here, Preston! I'm right here. You're not alone."

After the third or fourth time of reassuring Preston of my presence, I lay back down, cried, and whispered to God, "Lord, please heal my son! Please heal him." And in the still of the night, in the quietness of my bleeding momma-heart, my soul sensed Him whispering right back to me, *I'm right here, Gwen! I'm right here. For him. For you. You're not alone.*

Peace.

I heard the voice of Peace speak His presence and tenderness into my pain. He heard me. He knew of my plight. He knew I needed a word of encouragement. Not an audible word, just a heart whisper. He was right by my side. I knew it as I remembered His Word:

> The Lord is close to the brokenhearted and saves those who are crushed in spirit. (Psalm 34:18)

> O Lord, you have searched me and known me!
> You know when I sit down and when I rise up;
> you discern my thoughts from afar.
> You search out my path and my lying down
> and are acquainted with all my ways.
> Even before a word is on my tongue,
> behold, O Lord, you know it altogether.

You hem me in, behind and before,
    and lay your hand upon me.
Such knowledge is too wonderful for me;
    it is high; I cannot attain it.
Where shall I go from your Spirit?
    Or where shall I flee from your presence?
If I ascend to heaven, you are there!
    If I make my bed in Sheol, you are there!
If I take the wings of the morning
    and dwell in the uttermost parts of the sea,
even there your hand shall lead me,
    and your right hand shall hold me. (Psalm 139:1–10, ESV)

But as for me, the nearness of God is my good;
I have made the Lord GOD my refuge,
    that I may tell of all Your works. (Psalm 73:28, NASB)

Draw near to God and He will draw near to you. (James 4:8, NASB)

Peace.

Sometimes our heavy heart-burdens cry so loudly that we struggle to hear the voice of Peace and to remember the unsearchable, inescapable presence of God. At times our prayers seem to go unanswered, and our broken situations seem unfixable and painful. Oh, so painful!

We can't get through this life without knowing ache. But we don't face that pain alone. The Bible says that not a tear falls from our eyes that isn't known to God (Psalm 56:8).

He knows all about your heart-burdens.

He knows because He is the *omnipresent* God. That means He is present at all places at all times. This characteristic is unique to Him because all other created beings are limited by space and time. The *Holman Illustrated Bible Dictionary* has this to say about the omnipresence of God: "King David realized that there was nowhere he could go to escape God's presence (Ps. 139:7–12), and no conditions such as darkness could hide him from God. Even though God is present everywhere, He is not perceived everywhere. He can be fully present and yet hidden from the eyes of creatures, or He can make His presence felt either in blessing or judgment."[19]

This omnipresent characteristic of God is first seen in the Bible when Jacob announced his fresh awareness of God's presence. "Then Jacob awoke from his sleep and said, 'Surely the LORD is in this place, and I did not know it'" (Genesis 28:16, ESV). Has your heart ever been quickened to an awareness of God? Surely He is with you, friend, no matter where you find yourself in life today. There is no place you can go that God is not present. And though at times you may feel isolated, the Word of God reveals that you are never alone.

Hear this word of encouragement. Hear His whisper now. Whispers from His Word, from His heart:

I will never leave you or forsake you. I know your name and have engraved it on the palm of My hand. I hold your tears in a bottle and ache with you. My grace is sufficient, and I have told you these things, so that in Me you may have peace. In this world you will have trouble. But take heart! I have overcome the world. I'm right here. (Deuteronomy 31:6; Psalm 139; Isaiah 49:16; Psalm 56:8; 2 Corinthians 12:9; John 16:33)

Let's Pray

All-Present Lord, thanks for reminding me that You are always with me, that You see me, and that You hear my prayers. Please help me to know deeper levels of peace today in light of Your constant presence. In Jesus's name, amen.

The God Who Sees

El Roi

Sharon Jaynes

Today's Truth

She gave this name to the LORD who spoke to her: "You are the God who sees me [El Roi]," for she said, "I have now seen the One who sees me." (Genesis 16:13)

Friend to Friend

One day I was sitting on the patio with my friend Beth and her stepfather, Sam, as we waited for the grill to heat up before placing steaks on to cook. Beth's mom opened the door and gave Sam his orders, telling him what to do and how to do it. When she went back inside, Sam made a hand signal, pointing in one ear and out the other. We all three laughed.

Then he placed his ruddy hand on my friend's arm, a hand worn by years of working under the hoods of cars of every shape and size. "She was pretty hard on you growing up, wasn't she?" he asked.

"You have no idea," she answered with a sigh.

But he did have an idea. He understood. And that one simple gesture let her know that Sam had peered into her heart and had seen the truth. The weathered country mechanic had looked under the hood of her heart with the wisdom of the learned and seen the damaged and maimed engine within. A heart, though healed by Christ, that still felt the phantom pain of a little girl who was never good enough, who was constantly told what to do and how to do it—and who never felt she did it quite right. Sam saw her heart, and for that, Beth loved him. And so did I.[20]

One of my favorite names of God is El Roi, the God Who Sees. He sees your pain, feels your suffering, and understands your sorrow. He sees what you are going through. He sees you.

The first person to call God by the name El Roi was Hagar. A woman used. Abused. Tossed away. Driven away. Running away. She was all that and more.

Hagar was a maidservant, a girl slave to her mistress, Sarai. She had a job to do, and we have no indication that it was unpleasant, until a turn of events changed her life forever.

God came to Abram, Sarai's husband, and gave him some amazing news.

> Lift up your eyes from where you are and look north and south, east and west. All the land that you see I will give to you and your offspring forever. I will make your offspring like the dust of the earth, so that if anyone could count the dust, then your offspring could be counted....
>
> A son coming from your own body will be your heir. (Genesis 13:14–16; 15:4)

Abram told Sarai of God's promises, but as the months turned into years, Sarai grew impatient with God and His promises. "The Lord has kept me from having children," she complained to Abram.

"Go, sleep with my maidservant; perhaps I can build a family though her" (Genesis 16:2).

Oh my, this seems more than strange. But in those days, it was common practice for an infertile wife to offer her maid in order to keep the family name alive. So Abram bowed to his beautiful wife's bidding and bedded her maid. Hagar conceived a child—and a bit of pride to go with it. Then, in a way only a conniving woman can contrive, Sarai turned around and blamed Abram for the tension this pregnancy birthed. As Hagar's belly began to fill out, Sarai's jealousy began to well up.

> Then Sarai said to Abram, "You are responsible for the wrong I am suffering. I put my servant in your arms, and now that she knows she is pregnant, she despises me. May the LORD judge between you and me."
>
> "Your servant is in your hands," Abram said. "Do with her whatever you think best." (Genesis 16:5–6)

Sarai mistreated Hagar until she could bear it no more. You can imagine the cutting remarks. Angry words. Condemning looks. Finally, Hagar ran away to the desert.

As the discouraged woman lay languishing in the wilderness, the angel of the Lord came up beside her and asked the same question God asks all of us—a question akin to the first question He asked Adam and Eve in the garden (Genesis 3:9): "Where have you come from, and where are you going?" (Genesis 16:8). Of course God knew where she had come from and where she was going, but He also knew Hagar needed to say the words, just as we need to say the words.

"I'm running away from my mistress Sarai," the abused Hagar replied (verse 8).

"I'm running away from this lifeless marriage," the neglected wife decides.

"I'm running away from the pressures of this job," the man with the bottle responds.

"I'm running away from that cold-hearted woman," the man peering at porn justifies.

"I'm running away from these ungrateful children," the shop-aholic mother answers.

"I'm running away from the daily grind, endless chores, and piles of laundry," the lonely housewife sighs as she clicks on an old boyfriend's Facebook page.

"I'm running away..."

> Then the angel of the LORD told her, "Go back to your mistress and submit to her.... I will so increase your descendants that they will be too numerous to count.... The LORD has heard of your misery." (verses 9–11)

Hagar was a slave who had been sexually used and verbally abused. Hagar was a woman amazed that God heard her cries and saw her misery, that He took note of her condition and actually spoke to her.

Falling on her face, Hager gave God the name El Roi, the God Who Sees. "I have now seen the One who sees me," she cried (verse 13). She had heard God. She had seen God. More important, God had seen Hagar. God had heard Hagar.

What hope this scene offers for all of us! How incredibly reassuring to know that the Creator of the universe sees me, hears me, takes note of me, and speaks to me—and to you.

Hagar returned to her mistress, gave birth to a son, and placed him into Abram's arms. Fourteen years later, God was true to His word, and Sarai gave birth to a son of her own. (God also changed Abram's name to Abraham and Sarai's to Sarah.) When Abraham was one hundred years old and Sarah ninety, with a womb that was as good as dead, she birthed a bouncing baby boy whom they named Isaac. But rather than diminish Sarah's angst toward Hagar, the tension between the two boys stoked the fire of jealousy into full blaze.

On the day of Isaac's weaning party, Sarah demanded that Hagar and her son, Ishmael, be sent away for good. After wandering around in the desert, after their water supply had dried up, after giving up all hope, Hagar placed Ishmael under a tree to die. He cried. She cried. God heard.

> The angel of God called to Hagar from heaven and said to her, "What is the matter, Hagar? Do not be afraid; God has heard the boy crying as he lies there. Lift the boy up and take him by the hand, for I will make him into a great nation."
>
> Then God opened her eyes and she saw a well of water. (Genesis 21:17–19)

That last verse catches my breath every time. The water was there all the time, but she didn't see it. Not until *God opened* her eyes did the life-giving drink come into focus.

Sometimes, I feel just like Hagar. Not that I have ever truly been abused, but I have been tossed away when my usefulness was no longer needed. I've felt the sting of rejection, the pain of neglect, and the ache of loneliness. I have run away. And God has rescued me.

I'm also like Hagar in that, amid the crisis of the moment, I forget God's past faithfulness. God comes to me in my running away. He sees me. He notices me. I know He sees me. I call Him El Roi, and all is well. But time passes, as fourteen years passed for Hagar, and I forget. I forget what He has done for me, what He has said to me, what He has meant to me. I forget. I close my eyes and stumble about, thirsty again. I give up. I lay my hopes and dreams under a tree and walk away, leaving them to die.

Then comes a familiar voice. *What is the matter, Sharon? Do not be afraid; God has heard your crying.* And God woos me back once again. He opens my eyes to the well of living water that has been there all along.

Today, remember. Remember who God is and that He will do what He said He will do. He is El Roi, the God who sees me. He is the God who sees you.

Let's Pray

El Roi, thank You for seeing me, for hearing me, for rescuing me in my time of need. Help me to remember that there is nothing in my life that You don't see and nothing that You can't fix. Keep my eyes open to Your well of provision…the living water of Jesus Christ. In Jesus's name, amen.

My Hope

Miqweh Yisrael

Gwen Smith

Today's Truth

For you have been my hope, O Sovereign Lord, my confidence since my youth. (Psalm 71:5)

Friend to Friend

My girlfriend is caught between faith and a hard place. Even as a committed Christ follower, she struggles to believe God's promises and feels helpless because of her circumstances. She prays, but wonders if God hears her. She looks for a light at the end of the trial tunnel, yet sees nothing but shadows.

I think we've all been there at one time or another. I sure have. Are you, or is someone you love, there now? Without a doubt, God's ways and timing are mysterious, at times even frustrating. And the things He allows into our lives can be painful. Our hurting hearts cry out, *Are You even up there? Can You hear me? Do You care?*

Even in our darkest days, we know that God is still good, but waiting on Him can be *such* a difficult spiritual discipline.

The Bible features beautiful pictures of God's faithfulness to those who wait on Him. For example, the snapshots of God's might as displayed in the life of Elijah are simply fascinating. (Got a moment? Pause to read chapters 17 and 18 of 1 Kings now.) Elijah was the most dramatic and famous of all of Israel's prophets. God worked through him powerfully and miraculously, but Elijah sure did go through some serious seasons of waiting and wondering—just like my girlfriend. Just like each of us.

For years, Ahab (king of Israel) and his wife, Jezebel, had done evil in the eyes of the Lord. They worshiped Baal, an idol, instead of the one true God, which provoked the Lord to anger. *God. Was. Mad!* So He summoned Elijah to the scene. Elijah told Ahab, "As the LORD, the God of Israel, lives, whom I serve, there will be neither dew nor rain in the next few years except at my word" (1 Kings 17:1). As you can imagine, Ahab wasn't happy about the situation, and in his fury, he wanted Elijah dead. Yikes! But God had other plans. He spoke hope to Elijah's heart as He directed, protected, and provided for him throughout the time of the drought.

Oh yeah. Did I mention that the drought was three years long?

Three years.

This was not a simple and short situation, y'all.

In the third year, the Lord sent Elijah back to King Ahab, and a showdown of showdowns took place on Mount Carmel. A celestial boxing match began, with Baal and his false prophets in one corner, God and Elijah in the other. The bell rang, and the opponents danced from their corners to the center of the ring. The prophets of Baal took the first swing. They made a sacrifice to their god and cried out to him for hours, begging him to consume their offering with fire. Baal was silent and unresponsive, because he was not real. *Duh.*

Elijah knew he served a powerful, living, and responsive God, so he advanced to the center of the ring and took his swings with confidence. He repaired the altar of God, prepared the sacrifice, and then prayed for God to reveal His power. God flexed His divine muscles and answered Elijah's prayers instantly with an all-consuming fire. *Knockout!*

After the showdown was over, God told Elijah to deliver a new message to King Ahab. "And Elijah said to Ahab, 'Go, eat and drink, for there is the sound of a heavy rain'" (1 Kings 18:41). So Ahab went to eat, and Elijah went up to the top of Mount Carmel to look for evidence of God's rain miracle.

> "Go and look toward the sea," he told his servant. And he went up and looked.
>
> "There is nothing there," he said.
>
> Seven times Elijah said, "Go back."
>
> The seventh time the servant reported, "A cloud as small as a man's hand is rising from the sea." (verses 43–44)

What struck me as I studied this passage is that Elijah did not get his miracle right away this time. He had to wait and hope on the Lord. Could God have opened up the sky and poured out a storm immediately? You bet. Did He? No. Elijah had to wait. His servant had to look for the miracle...and look...and look...and look.

Seven times.

No disrespect to Elijah, but doesn't that perk your heart up? Even God's superstar prophet had to wait on God's timing.

You and I are not the only ones who have to wait and hope, friend! God's will is God's will. It bends for no man. Yet ours can bend to His. When we submit to His perfect plan, we will find the hope we are looking for, even in the waiting—or perhaps especially in the waiting.

> Meanwhile, the sky grew black with clouds, the wind rose, a heavy rain came on. (verse 45)

God moved. Once again, He was faithful. His character requires it.

Now consider this: God used Elijah in really big ways. Elijah spoke on God's behalf, he was God's front-line man in raising a dead child back to life in order to bless a widowed mother, and he was the lead character in a miraculous God show that brought fire from heaven, consuming an offering and connecting the hearts of wandering people back to the heart of God. We're talking *big* God stuff! Yet even Elijah experienced difficult situations and was forced to wait on God.

Looking back, I now realize that God has strengthened my hope muscles most in the seasons when I've had to wait on Him. God is Miqweh Yisrael, which is Hebrew for "the Hope of Israel." Israel looked to Miqweh Yisrael for deliverance, salvation, protection, provision, and direction. We look to Him with the same sense of expectation, for He is the hope of *all* who trust Him, all who belong to Him.

Do you hope in Him? If you sometimes struggle to nurture hope, you are in good company. In his hard time, the author of Psalm 42 had to remind himself where to place his hope. He had to choose to praise.

> Why are you downcast, O my soul?
>   Why so disturbed within me?

Put your hope in God,
for I will yet praise him,
my Savior and my God. (Psalm 42:5–6)

Sometimes you and I have to remind ourselves that God is our hope. We have to remind ourselves to look to Him as Miqweh Yisrael. Like the psalmist, we might need to throw down some determined praise.

I don't like waiting. I imagine you don't either. I take solace that Jesus gives us hope in the midst of it: "In this world you will have trouble. But take heart! I have overcome the world" (John 16:33). His promises bring hope.

> So God has given both his promise and his oath. These two things are unchangeable because it is impossible for God to lie. Therefore, we who have fled to him for refuge can have great confidence as we hold to the hope that lies before us. This hope is a strong and trustworthy anchor for our souls. It leads us through the curtain into God's inner sanctuary. Jesus has already gone in there for us. He has become our eternal High Priest in the order of Melchizedek. (Hebrews 6:18–20, NLT)

Jesus *is* our Hope.

When discouragement sets in and you feel unheard, when you are forced to wait on God, when you find yourself caught between faith and a hard place, when there is nothing there—no evidence of God's miracle on the horizon—remember that God is faithful, powerful, and responsive. He has seen you through trials in the past, and

He will see you through trials in the future. Even in the challenges you face now, you are seen, you are heard. Choose to trust Him as Miqweh Yisrael, the God of your Hope.

> May the God of hope fill you with all joy and peace as you trust in him, so that you may overflow with hope by the power of the Holy Spirit. (Romans 15:13)

Let's Pray

Dear Lord, Miqweh Yisrael, my Hope, I worship You, the one true God! You are mighty and powerful, full of never-ending compassion and love. Please help me to see You when I face trials and to trust Your heart when circumstances discourage me. In Jesus's name, amen.

The Lord Who Heals
Yahweh Rapha

Mary Southerland

Today's Truth

He [the Lord] said, "If you listen carefully to the voice of the Lord your God and do what is right in his eyes, if you pay attention to his commands and keep all his decrees, I will not bring on you any of the diseases I brought on the Egyptians, for I am the Lord, who heals you." (Exodus 15:26)

Friend to Friend

We all need healing at various times in our lives—physical, emotional, moral, or relational healing. We are broken people living in a broken world. We are frail humans and will battle illnesses of all kinds until we get to heaven. Until then, we have a choice to make. We can embrace our illness, no matter what form it takes, and trust Yahweh Rapha, the Lord Who Heals, to bring healing and restoration in His own way and in His perfect timing. Or we can choose to do what I often do: whine and complain, just like the Israelites.

After God miraculously provided for the Israelites by parting the Red Sea, they continued on their journey. The living conditions were not quite what they had expected, and the lack of water was a problem. Get this: they went *three whole days* with no water after witnessing one of God's greatest miracles! When they came to Marah and found water, their delight soon turned once again to grumbling when they discovered that the water was bitter (Exodus 15:22–24).

Moses didn't panic. He simply prayed. God instructed him to cast a tree into the water, and the water became sweet. God then told the Israelites that He is Yahweh Rapha, "the LORD, who heals you" (verse 26). Interesting! The Israelites were not sick. They were thirsty. Why did God reveal Himself to them as Yahweh Rapha, the Lord Who Heals?

The Hebrews had suffered terribly in Egypt and were thrilled to leave the bondage of Pharaoh, but freedom didn't usher them into a life of ease. They had to rely on God for everything, and when their circumstances were less than ideal, their hearts filled with resentment. God knew their greatest need was not water. What they really needed was healing from bitterness and pain, and He longed to bring that healing to them. But the Israelites continued to complain about their circumstances and wanted to return to Egypt. What in the world was wrong with them?

They suffered from the same ailments that plague you and me: pride, fear, and a desire for control. We sometimes find it easier to stay in the pit than to struggle toward the light of freedom. Freedom is expensive, demands obedience, and requires a willingness to abandon ourselves to God.

I had almost forgotten what it felt like to wake up at the bottom of that ugly pit called clinical depression. The darkness had been a familiar companion for most of my life. Over the years, I'd tried just about everything to soothe the pain in my heart and mind—things like success in ministry, the approval of others, perfectionism, doing good things, and food, to name a few. But in 1995, the bottom fell out of my life, and I spent two long years climbing out of that pit of darkness. God lovingly redefined me and gave me a new song to sing as He opened doors for me to speak to women across the world about how to find hope in the midst of depression. I have often said, "I would go through that pit experience again tomorrow because of what God has done in my life through it." I truly meant those words. I just didn't think that "tomorrow" would really come. But it did.

I underwent what I believed would be a simple medical procedure, but when I woke up in recovery, I knew I was in trouble. The doctor said the surgery went well, but that she had not expected to find so much scar tissue and repair work to do. I certainly hadn't expected the level of pain and helplessness that overwhelmed me. Those ten days I had so generously carved out of my schedule turned into months of painful and slow recovery. I could feel myself sliding into that familiar pit of darkness.

Like the Israelites, I have a problem with pride, obedience, and wholly trusting God and His plan for true and ultimate healing. I was raised to be strong and independent and find it hard to accept help. When people asked how they could lend a hand during my recovery, my automatic response was, "I'm fine. I'll let you know if I need anything." Fortunately, my family and friends ignored that absurd assertion and stepped right over my pride as they brought meals, cleaned house, did laundry, assumed my teaching and speaking responsibilities, and kept our infant grandson while our daughter attended school three days a week. I couldn't even get out of bed or go downstairs without help—and I did not like it one bit! In fact, I was furious! And just as a tiny spark can flame into a raging fire, unresolved anger can flare into depression.

At that point, I had a choice to make—a choice we each face at some point, because pain and darkness will surely come into our lives. We can choose to become bitter and blame God, or we can wallow in the mire and mud of the slimy pit into which we have fallen. I am often guilty of plastering a smile on my face, gritting my teeth, and denying that the pit even exists. However, the choice we *should* make is to trust God, knowing He is Yahweh Rapha and will heal us and give us the strength to endure whatever trial we face. The apostle Paul understood and lived out the truth of trusting God:

> To keep me from becoming conceited because of these surpassingly great revelations, there was given me a thorn in my flesh, a messenger of Satan, to torment me. Three times I pleaded with the Lord to take it away from me. But he said to me, "My grace is sufficient for you, for my power is made perfect in weakness." Therefore I will boast all the more gladly about my weaknesses, so that Christ's power may rest on me. (2 Corinthians 12:7–9)

Paul was an expert at squeezing a seed of victory and truth out of every tough circumstance. He did not sin in asking God to remove his affliction, but when the answer was no, he chose wholehearted surrender to the Healer's plan. Paul may not have understood God's process, but he knew God's heart and wholly trusted Him. God was sending Paul a message of hope. It is important to note the tense of the verb in this verse: *But he said to me* can be translated "he [God] has once-for-all said to me." It is an eternal promise.

The story is told of a businessman who was selling warehouse property that had been empty for months. Since vandals had damaged doors, smashed windows, and left garbage, the building needed expensive repairs. As the owner showed a prospective buyer the property, he quickly explained that he would make any repairs needed. The buyer said, "Forget the repairs. I'm going to build something completely different. I don't want the building, just the site." So too our God restores and rebuilds. From the rubble of our past, He builds a new life—a better life.

God's grace tears down the old prison walls and sets the prisoners free. He turns defeat into victory, tragedy into triumph, and weakness into strength by providing His power over circumstances. That is true healing—the eternal healing power of God!

People without Christ can muster up enough courage and human strength to get through a trial. But God will not only enable us to survive the hard times, He will empower us to thrive in and because of them. Paul used his pain as an opportunity to trust and obey God. We can do the same as we trust the healing power of Yahweh Rapha.

Let's Pray

Father, thank You that You are my strength and my joy at a time when I feel so weak, trapped in a pit of despair. By faith, I turn to You and seek Your forgiveness for the pride that blinds me to the hope I can find in You. Please help me to see Your hand at work in my life, and even when I can't, give me the power to walk by faith and not by sight. You are my God. You are my everything. You are my Yahweh Rapha. In Jesus's name, amen.

Day 5

The Lord Is There
Yahweh Shammah

Sharon Jaynes

Today's Truth

And the name of the city from that time on will be: THE LORD IS THERE [Yahweh Shammah]. (Ezekiel 48:35)

Friend to Friend

Steve and I got married when we were both still in college. He was entering his fourth year of dental school, and I was just a few hours shy of completing my degree. The last year of school held many important decisions for us, such as where Steve would set up his practice. Dentists don't tend to move about, so this was an important, probably lifelong, decision for both of us.

All year we prayed, researched, and weighed various opportunities and options. Finally, in April of that year, we felt God calling us to Pineville, North Carolina, right outside Charlotte. A dentist there was looking for a young associate, and the pieces of the puzzle began falling into place. We had prayed. We had fasted. We had listened. We felt that this was God's answer for our lives. It was a big deal.

So after graduation, we packed our meager belongings and moved to Charlotte. After setting up house in our tiny apartment, Steve went to meet the dentist whose practice he was joining so that they could finalize the work schedule and management particulars.

"Steve, I've been thinking about it," the doctor began, "and I don't think this is such a good idea after all. I've changed my mind." He extended his hand to my twenty-five-year-old stunned husband and said, "Good luck to you, son."

I was surprised when Steve came home much earlier than I expected. "What are you doing home?" I asked.

"Sit down," he said, somehow managing to sound calm. "You're not going to believe this."

Steve told me the story and I was shocked. A host of raw emotions collided with questions for God. *How could You do this? How could we have been so wrong? Didn't we hear You correctly? Have You gone on vacation and forgotten about us? Where are You? We prayed. We fasted. We wanted nothing more than to do what You wanted us to do where You wanted us to do it. Now here we sit in a big city, with a big student loan, and no job. Now what are we supposed to do?*

A flood of doubts burst through the dam of my faith, and I felt the waters rising.

In the book of Ezekiel, the nation of Israel was in a tough situation—again. God's chosen people seemed to continually ride the Ferris wheel of rebellion and repentance. They started at the top with intimacy with God, descended with rebellion against God, sunk to the bottom with punishment by God for the purpose of drawing them back, followed by the upward climb of repentance and renewed intimacy with God. Around and around they went, cycling through the stages time and time again.

Now the Israelites were once more in the punishment stage.

They had rebelled against God and done what was right in their own eyes. As a result, He allowed them to be taken into Babylonian captivity for seventy years (Jeremiah 29:10). The glory of the Lord had departed from the temple (Ezekiel 10:18–19; 11:22–24), and it was a dark, dismal time for the rebellious nation. However, in the last verse of Ezekiel's prophetic book, God gives them the promise of hope for the future. "My dwelling place will be with them; I will be their God, and they will be my people. Then the nations will know that I the LORD make Israel holy, when my sanctuary is among them forever.... The name of the city from that time on will be: THE LORD IS THERE [Yahweh Shammah]" (Ezekiel 37:27–28; 48:35).

The Hebrew word *shammah* simply means "there."[21] And while Ezekiel 48:35 actually describes the name of a city, it is also commonly referred to as a name of God.

How precious that God sent His Son and gave Him the name Immanuel, "God with us" (Matthew 1:23). He will never leave us or forsake us (Hebrews 13:5). He is the Lord who is there, and He has a plan (Jeremiah 29:11).

Let's go back to what seemed like a career setback for Steve and me. It seems rather petty now that I'm older and aware of the tragic losses experienced by women who write to me every day. But I have discovered that the accumulations of petty disappointments tend to undermine our faith, like little termites gnawing away at the foundation of our trust. They can leave us doubting whether or not God is really concerned about the everyday details of our lives. As the ground beneath us seems to crumble, we wonder, *Why should I pray at all?*

Our limited vision doesn't allow us to see *how* God is working behind the scenes in our lives. But we must believe that He is. That's where trust comes in. The eighteenth-century writer Jean-Pierre de Caussade said it well:

> You would be very ashamed if you knew what experiences you call setbacks, upheavals, pointless disturbances, and tedious annoyances really are. You would realize that your complaints about them are nothing more nor less than blasphemies—though that never occurs to you. Nothing happens to you except by the will of God, and yet [God's] beloved children curse it because they do not know it for what it is.[22]

God's ways are higher than our ways and His thoughts higher than our thoughts (Isaiah 55:9). He is working, whether we recognize it or not.

Difficulties are pregnant with what I call moments of sudden glory—intimate moments when God makes His presence known. They are just waiting to be birthed in the lives of those willing to labor through the pain. The key is to not allow bitterness and anger to make our hearts infertile to Yahweh Shammah's gifts, because one day we will realize He was there all the time.

During the days that followed the doctor changing his mind about Steve joining his practice, we never went hungry. I worked six days a week in various dental offices, and Steve filled in where he could. Three months later, a situation opened up in a desirable part of town with one of the city's most respected doctors. Steve was offered a wonderful situation in which to begin his career. If we had written out the best-case scenario, it would not have come close to what God provided. It was Ephesians 3:20 in lab-coat white: "Now to him who is able to do immeasurably more than all we ask or imagine, according to his power that is at work within us."

After a few years, the part of town in which we originally had planned to set up Steve's practice became a rundown thoroughfare, and that other doctor's office eventually disappeared. I'm not even sure what happened to him. Meanwhile, Steve's practice continued to grow and grow and grow, until we had to move out on our own to expand. We experienced Yahweh Shammah's provision and protection through the twists and turns of uncertainty.

Well, why didn't God do that in the first place? Why didn't He lead us to that second opportunity when we did all that praying and seeking? He could have. But He is far more interested in developing our character than in doling out a life of comfort and ease. C. S. Lewis noted, "If you think of this world as a place intended simply for our happiness, you find it quite intolerable: think of it as a place of training and correction and it's not so bad."[23] We are ever the students. He is the teacher still. Trials rip away the flimsy fabric of self-sufficiency and become the raw material for God's miracles in our lives. And those miracles become moments of sudden glory—moments when God makes His presence and activity known in our lives, moments in which we recognize THE LORD IS THERE.

A year after this particular trial, I sat thanking God for His provision, and I was ashamed of myself. Ashamed that I had doubted God. Ashamed that I had fussed at Him. Ashamed that I had thrown a temper tantrum when I didn't get what I wanted when I wanted it—and I'm so glad I didn't.

"I'm so sorry, God," I prayed. "Please forgive me."

That's okay, He seemed to say. *Happens all the time. Now, I want this to be a lesson for you. You've got to trust Me.*

Philip Yancey once observed, "Faith means believing in advance what will only make sense in reverse."[24] Oh, that we would trust Him even if the twists and turns never make sense this side of heaven. That's what trusting God is all about. As we live and move and have our being in Him, the dark places become opportunities to trust that He knows the way and to hold on tight.

He is Yahweh Shammah, THE LORD IS THERE.[25]

Let's Pray

Yahweh Shammah, I am so thankful that You are in control. Help me to remember that You are always there. You will never leave me or forsake me, and I can trust You. There is no place I can go that is away from Your presence. In Jesus's name, amen.

Now It's Your Turn

Time for Reflection

This week we looked at the omnipresence of God, the fact that He is all present in all places at all times. Read Isaiah 43:1–3, 5: "But now, this is what the Lord says—he who created you, O Jacob, he who formed you, O Israel: 'Fear not, for I have redeemed you; I have summoned you by name; you are mine. When you pass through the waters, I will be with you; and when you pass through the rivers, they will not sweep over you. When you walk through the fire, you will not be burned; the flames will not set you ablaze. For I am the Lord, your God, the Holy One of Israel, your Savior.… Do not be afraid, for I am with you.'"

Identify in this passage the promises God made to His children and *personalize* them below. *Example:* God has redeemed me.

God has ______________________________________.

I am ____.

When I ______________________________________.

When I ______________________________________.

When I ______________________________________.

The flames ___________________________________.

God is ______________________________________.

- God spoke these promises to His people, the Israelites, through the prophet Isaiah. Just as He promised to be with them through each flood and fire of life, Scripture tells us that God will never leave us or forsake us either (Deuteronomy 31:8; Hebrews 13:5). Do you believe that this is the heart of God for all His children and that the statements above are true? Why or why not?

  How does this speak to the circumstances you face today? What does the omnipresence of God mean to you?
- God sees you and He knows your name. He was called El Roi, the God Who Sees, in Genesis 16 by a hurting slave girl named Hagar when she realized that the Lord of the universe cared for her plight and saw her as she tried to escape from her problems. Describe how Hagar must have been feeling both times she found herself in the desert—first when she ran away, next when she was sent away. Describe a circumstance when you felt the same way—even a circumstance that's prompting you to feel that way today.
- In Genesis 21:19 the eyes of Hagar were opened by God to see His provision and protection. In response to this divine revelation, "she went and filled the skin with water and gave the boy a drink." When God opens our eyes to see the well of His provision, protection, and persistent pursuit of our hearts, that gift is never for us alone. He calls us to fill our skins and give others a drink. Whom is God calling you to refresh today? What steps will you take to obey?
- As we read of God's intervention, protection, and power displayed through the prophet Elijah, we were reminded that God is the Hope of His people, Miqweh Yisrael. Elijah had to wait on and hope in God just as we do. When tough times come, we

have to remind ourselves to place our hope in God and trust Him to lead us through. Look up Psalm 25:4–5 and fill in the blanks below.

"______ ______ your ways, O Lord, ______ ______ your paths; ______ ______ in your truth and ______ ______, for you are God my Savior, and my hope is in you all day long."

What do you notice about all the sections you filled in? How is that relevant to your spiritual growth? In what way do these heart requests affect your ability to place your hope in God alone each day?

- We also looked at the Lord Who Heals (Yahweh Rapha) and the Lord Is There (Yahweh Shammah) this week. It's true that pain, illnesses, and pits of every kind can bring life as we know it to a screeching halt. At such times we'll find it beneficial to ask God to change our perspective on our challenges and then to examine our priorities in light of that new perspective. Read 1 Peter 1:3–7. Compare your perspective to the one described in these verses.
- Wrap up your response time with prayer. Move from confession, to adoration, to thanksgiving, and end with your petitions (personal prayer needs).

Going Deeper with God

List: the attributes and names of God with their meanings that were covered this week.

1.
2.
3.

4. ____
5. ____

Read and pray: Go back and read the story of Hagar in Genesis 21. Zoom in on verse 19: "Then God opened her eyes and she saw a well of water." The well was there all along. She just didn't see it. Today, pray that God will open your eyes to His provision and protection in your life.

Write and memorize: Psalm 25:4–5. Let this become your heart's prayer.

____

____

____

Worship: Allow the song "The One Who Sees Me" to be a response of worship from your heart to the heart of God right now. You can listen to it here: www.girlfriendsingod.com/2012/worship-the-one-who-sees-me/.

Your GiG *Knowing God by Name* Journal

Spend a few moments contemplating and journaling about some of the scriptural truths that moved your heart as you read the devotions this week. Then use the space below to collect your thoughts or write a prayer of response to God.

____

____

____

3-31-16

JoAnn Hood - Lung cancer metasticized

Arlon Boatman

Paul Pustejovsky

Diane Pritchard

Lon Jorgenson

Helen & John Rambo

Debbie's Dad

Brandon White

Barrett's - Bev's deceased grandson

3rd ~~anniversary~~ anniversary

Fear not, for…I have summoned you by name; you are mine. When you pass through the waters, I will be with you. (Isaiah 43:1–2)

Day 1

My Stronghold and My Strong Tower

Migdal-Oz

Mary Southerland

Today's Truth

The Lord is a refuge for the oppressed, a stronghold in times of trouble. Those who know your name will trust in you, for you, Lord, have never forsaken those who seek you. (Psalm 9:9–10)

Friend to Friend

We live in Kansas City, where summers typically include some fierce thunderstorms. Our three-year-old grandson, Justus, is not a fan. The driving rain, loud thunder, and often violent lightning frighten him. We have tried to reassure Justus with such logical explanations as the thunder is nothing more than God rearranging the furniture in heaven and lightning is just the angels setting off fireworks. I know. He didn't buy our imaginative reassurances either.

Justus sleeps over at our house one night a week to give his mom and dad the opportunity to have some kid-free time together. At least that's the excuse we give them. We also keep him to get our "Justus fix." You see, Justus is a special little boy, a walking hunk of joy who lights up the world and makes you feel like you are the most important part of that world.

One day after picking up Justus for our weekly date, we got caught in a torrential downpour, a particularly brutal storm. As the thunder roared and the lightning crashed, Justus tightly clamped both of his little hands over his ears and squeezed his eyes shut as hard as he could, hoping to block out the frightening sounds and sights of the scary storm.

Dan and I kept reassuring Justus that the storm would pass and we'd soon be safely home. Dan said, "Buddy, it's really okay!"

But it was *not* okay with Justus. In frustration and fear, he finally turned to his grandfather and exclaimed, "Papa, can't you *do* something! Can't you *pwease* turn down the *stowm*?"

My husband turned to Justus and said, "Honey, I can't turn down the storm, but you are with Mimi and Papa, so everything really is going to be okay. We love you and we'll take care of you. You are safe with us."

Justus thought for a moment before his beautiful face broke into a peace-filled smile and he said, "Okay, Papa." With a sigh, he leaned back in his car seat and promptly fell asleep. Justus had found his stronghold, his safe place where he could peacefully rest while the storm was raging.

In the Old Testament, God is referred to as "Strong Tower" or "a Stronghold." The Hebrew word is *Migdal-Oz.* Strongholds are essentially fortified defensive structures or any position of strength and safety. Strongholds have been used throughout history to provide refuge from enemies and from the storms of life. In biblical times, some cities were enclosed by walls twenty-five feet high and fifteen to twenty-five feet thick. Farmers worked in the fields by day and then retreated within the city walls at night for safety and protection. Many wars were won because the enemy was unable to break down or through the stronghold's defenses. Strongholds provided safety from enemies and protected the food supply. Enemies could wreak havoc on a town without a stronghold.

King David, a great warrior, was gifted in battle and understood the importance of having a place of refuge—a stronghold. We see through his bold declaration in Psalm 9 that he also understood the importance of having a spiritual stronghold—not a building or structure, but God. David found his strength and protection in God, and in God alone he put his trust. Later, in Psalm 18:2, David wrote, "The LORD is my rock, my fortress and my deliverer; my God is my rock, in whom I take refuge. He is my shield and the horn of my salvation, my stronghold."

When the storms of life hit, David found safety in God alone. We can do the same.

I have a friend who loves to sail. When I asked if he had ever been caught in a bad storm, he responded, "Many times!"

I shook my head in disbelief, concluding that he was obviously a glutton for punishment. Of course, I had to ask, "Then why do you keep sailing?"

His answer was profound. "Mary, every sailor knows that there will be storms. You just learn what to do when the storm hits. In a severe storm, there is only one thing to do and only one way to survive. You have to put the ship in a certain position and keep her there."

The same is true in our lives. When the storms of life overwhelm us, there is only one thing to do if we want to survive. We must position ourselves in the right place. We must place ourselves in the hands of God, our stronghold, and He will keep us safely there until the storm has passed. Consider the confidence and hope expressed by the psalmist in these words: "He stilled the storm to a whisper; the waves of the sea were hushed" (Psalm 107:29). We really can trust God to bring peace and to reduce the fiercest storm to a mere whisper. The faithful provision and sustaining comfort of God at work in our lives depend on the character and heart of God and our willingness to trust Him.

Author and theologian Richard Fuller wrote:

> This, Christian, is what you must do. Sometimes, like Paul, you can see neither sun nor stars, and no small tempest lies on you....
>
> Reason cannot help you; past experiences give you no light.... Only a single course is left. You must put your soul in one position and keep it there.
>
> You must stay upon the Lord; and come what may—winds, waves, cross seas, thunder, lightning, frowning rocks, roaring breakers—no matter what, you must lash yourself to the helm, and hold fast your confidence in God's faithfulness, His covenant engagement, His everlasting love in Christ Jesus.[26]

What peace we can have, knowing God has gone before us through every valley, across each mountain of life. He knows what tomorrow holds and will give us everything we need to face it. When we begin to understand and live in the certainty that God monitors every circumstance, we will walk in victory, knowing God really is in control.

We can face every storm with confidence, knowing God will redeem it for good if we run to Him and, like David, declare Him to be our stronghold. A stronghold is useless if we are standing outside its walls. We need to stop trying to weather the storms of life on our own. We are not alone. God is with us, waiting for us to enter His fortress of refuge. We can trust few things in this life, but God's faithfulness is one of them. When the hard times come and the storms roll in, place yourself in God's safekeeping. Run to your Strong Tower of Refuge.

I have often prayed the same request our grandson made: "God, can You *please* turn down the storm in my life? Can't You make the thunderous chaos go away? And the flashing pain is so hard to handle, Lord. I am scared!" You may find yourself in a frightening place filled with darkness and doubt. Your wounded heart may be wondering if God knows where you are. He does. You think that because you cannot see the hand of God or sense His presence, it means He isn't working. Nothing could be further from the truth. God is *always* at work in our lives. Be assured, God really is in control, and nothing can get to you without going through Him. You can trust fully and rest confidently in your stronghold.

Let's Pray

Father, when the darkness comes and doubt invades, I sometimes complain that I don't understand and cannot see Your hand at work. Forgive me for my demanding and faithless attitude. Forgive me for not trusting You. Help me, by the power of Your Spirit, to trust You completely. Lord, thank You for Your faithfulness to me. You alone are my stronghold and all is well. In Jesus's name, amen.

God My Strength

El Sali

Gwen Smith

Today's Truth

I love you, O LORD, my strength. (Psalm 18:1, ESV)

Friend to Friend

I will never forget how the movie *The Wizard of Oz* lingered in my heart for days after I first saw it. I was just a child like the heroine Dorothy, who won me over the instant she effortlessly sang the dreamy lines of "Over the Rainbow." I was moved profoundly by the story of this young girl who had been caught up in a complicated dog matter and a whirling tornado that transported her to a strange and bewildering land far from home.

While watching the adventure play out on television, I joined the story in my imagination. I cheered for Dorothy as she came to the defense of her spirited puppy, Toto, when a witchy woman wanted him killed. I sank deep into the couch cushions and trembled with fear when the black-and-white farmhouse was lifted in a storm, then crashed down in an unfamiliar place of Technicolor.

Along the yellow brick road, I made friends when Dorothy made friends. Never again would I look at a scarecrow, a lion, or a tin can the same way! I shared in her longing for a safe return home to her auntie Em and their farm in Kansas. My heart-hopes soared with hers as Dorothy was told of a powerful man in the Emerald City who could help her: the Wizard of Oz!

As with any good story, there were scary struggles and frustrating setbacks. Flying monkeys captured Dorothy and her friends, and a wicked witch set out to destroy her. Even so, determined Dorothy continued on the yellow brick road toward the Emerald City because she'd placed her hopes in the powers possessed by the famed Wizard of Oz.

Sadly, after persevering through all the dangerous predicaments, Dorothy and her friends found out that the wizard was, in fact, powerless. Powerless! What a stinkin' disappointment! Dorothy was crushed. Her buddies were crushed. I was crushed. How in the world could this happen? Hope had skipped alongside them for the entire journey down the yellow brick road. How could anticipated strength possibly fade to weakness?

Alas, it did.

Hearts were heavy with the ache of disappointment. All seemed lost.

Then a surprising shimmer of hope broke through: Dorothy actually possessed the power that she needed to get home. In fact, she'd had the power all along. Her ruby-red slippers were the key!

Woo-hoo!

Let me just say, at this point happy dances were thrown down on both the screen and in my living room.

Tears fell as good-byes and hugs were shared. Then Dorothy grabbed Toto and made her way home by calling on the power that had been with her all along. Within seconds, the Kansas girl found herself back over the rainbow of a dream, safe and sound at home.

To this day, that story still moves me.

I can relate to Dorothy on so many levels. She was a girl with a dream and a song in her heart. An average, ordinary girl who had to deal with complicated people and sort through difficult circumstances. A girl who knew how it felt to place her hopes in other people and be disappointed. A girl who finally came upon the strength she needed to find her way home.

Isn't that true for all of us?

Aren't we continually looking for the strength we need to bring our hopes into reality?

Moses too faced complicated challenges and whirling storms of circumstances. Born in a time when he, as a Hebrew baby boy, was supposed to have been killed, Moses was saved by God's sovereign grace when Pharaoh's daughter pulled him from the Nile and kept him as her own.

A Hebrew among Egyptians, Moses was raised in a land and culture that was far removed from his heritage and from the one true God of Israel, as far as black and white is from Technicolor.

You know this story! We saw it on the flannelgraph boards in Sunday school as little girls. We watched Charlton Heston act it out in the movie *The Ten Commandments.* Moses *had it all* in the palace, *lost it all* when he murdered an Egyptian soldier, then eventually *risked it all* for the holy God who called out to him and commissioned him from a flame. (Need a refresher course on the details? Go read the book of Exodus. It's completely amazing.)

Moses set out to free his people through the power of God. Though Pharaoh doubted God's strength, the Lord displayed His might, plague after plague, until finally it looked like Pharaoh got the memo. At last he let God's people go. Moses's yellow brick road of rescue led him and the Israelites out of Egypt. But when Pharaoh changed his mind and gathered his army to chase them, the Israelites ran smack-dab up against the Red Sea. Major problem.

Not one to be hindered by impossibility, the Lord took care of business in a huge and powerful way. He parted and held back the Red Sea for Moses and the Israelites so they could escape destruction and experience deliverance. After His people crossed over safely, God again demonstrated His strength by sweeping the pharaoh and his army into the sea, killing every last one of them (Exodus 13 and 14).

My goodness. What a story! What. A. God! Girl, if this doesn't get you excited about the strength of God, I'm not quite sure what will!

> Israel saw the great power that the LORD used against the Egyptians, so the people feared the LORD, and they believed in the LORD and in his servant Moses. (Exodus 14:31, ESV)

Then a big ol' party went down as Moses and the Israelites sang to the Lord a song that's commonly referred to as the song of Moses.

> The LORD is my strength and my song;
>   he has become my salvation.
> He is my God, and I will praise him,
>   my father's God, and I will exalt him. (Exodus 15:2)

In Exodus 15, Moses calls God his strength and celebrates the power that brought salvation to his people. As you may have picked up from yesterday's study of Migdal-Oz (Strong Tower), *oz* is a Hebrew word for "strength." How about that! But as we've seen already, the Bible reveals many names that highlight the power of our God; El Sali is a Hebrew name meaning "God of my Strength; God my

Rock."[27] King David also calls God his Strength, El Sali, in Psalm 59:9: "O my Strength, I watch for you; you, O God, are my fortress." Then again in verse 17, "O my Strength, I sing praise to you; you, O God, are my fortress, my loving God."

Elohei Ma'uzzi is another Hebrew name meaning "God of my Strength." As David sang, "It is God who arms me with strength and makes my way perfect" (2 Samuel 22:33).[28]

Are you experiencing the strength of God?

You might be struggling with this, wondering where God is in your story. Perhaps you find yourself lamenting to the God of Strength, El Sali, wondering why you've been forgotten and why you feel weak. Maybe things are good for you right now, but you know of others who have encountered setbacks along their yellow brick roads. Each of us is guaranteed life challenges, but God promises to be our strength when we call on Him. He is not a puffed-up and powerless wizard of Oz hiding behind a curtain, pulling strings. He is El Sali, the God of Strength who loves you and longs to move in and through your life.

Will you trust Him more deeply today and allow His joy to be your strength?

Let's Pray

Dear Lord, my Strength, El Sali, You are powerful and loving. Thank You for allowing me—this average, ordinary girl with complicated relationships and difficult circumstances—to have access to Your perfect strength when I am weak. Help me to trust You when all my heart sees are lions and tigers and bears. In Jesus's name, amen.

The Lord Is My Banner
Yahweh Nissi

Sharon Jaynes

Today's Truth

Moses built an altar and called it The Lord is my Banner [Yahweh Nissi]. (Exodus 17:15)

Friend to Friend

I'm going to be honest with you. If there were an Olympic event for feelings of insecurity, inferiority, and inadequacy, at some point my picture would have been on the Wheaties cereal box as the winner of a gold medal.

Now, you probably think I'm going to tell you, "But then I became a Christian and all that insecurity just went away!" But that's not completely true. I did become a Christian when I was fourteen. That part is correct. However, I carried that insecurity into my Christian life like a ball and chain clamped around my skinny ankle. Don't get me wrong; I could sing "Victory in Jesus" with the best of them. I knew without a shadow of a doubt that when I left the confines of this earth and crossed over the threshold into the eternal realm, I was going to be with Jesus forever. It was what I was supposed to do until I got there that had me stumped. I had no idea how to walk in victory in this life or what that even meant.

Did you know that you can be a bona fide, born-again Christian and still live in defeat? Yes, you can. But if you do, if *I* do, it's not God's fault. He has given us "everything we need for life and godliness through our knowledge of him who called us by his own glory and goodness" (2 Peter 1:3). He has equipped us with the power of the Holy Spirit (Acts 1:8), the mind of Christ (1 Corinthians 2:16), and the precious promises that never fail (2 Peter 1:4). But it's up to us to walk in the truth of who He is and who we are in Him. It is up to us to walk in victory as "more than conquerors" in Christ Jesus (Romans 8:37).

Moses had to deal with the same insecurities that you and I grapple with. As we learned earlier, Moses was a former prince of Egypt who became a runaway felon. For the next forty years, Moses took care of his father-in-law's sheep in the Midian desert. When he was eighty years old, God spoke to Moses through the burning bush. We looked at that conversation at the start of Week 2, but let's visit it one more time.

> The LORD said, "*I* have indeed seen the misery of my people in Egypt. *I* have heard them crying out because of their slave drivers, and *I* am concerned about their suffering. So *I* have come down to rescue them from the hand of the Egyptians and to bring them up out of that land into a good and spacious land, a land flowing with milk and honey—the home of the Canaanites, Hittites, Amorites, Perizzites, Hivites and Jebusites." (Exodus 3:7–8)

This was all sounding good to Moses—until God mentioned how He was going to bring all that about.

> So now, go. I am sending *you* to Pharaoh to bring my people the Israelites out of Egypt. (verse 10)

Deliverance for his people! This was what Moses had always wanted! But when God said, "I am sending you," Moses starting backing up. The three-headed monster of inferiority, insecurity, and inadequacy wrapped its talons around Moses's scruffy neck and began to squeeze.

Four times Moses told God why He had the wrong man for the job, and four times God reassured Moses that He was the Almighty God who was sufficient to do the job through him. It was a hard lesson for Moses. It has been a hard lesson for me. I wonder if it has been a hard lesson for you.

Of course, we know how the story goes. After several weeks of very persuasive plagues, Pharaoh did let God's people go. They crossed the Red Sea on dry land, ate manna that fell from heaven, drank water that sprang from a rock, and roasted quail that rained from the sky.

Not too far into their journey to the Promised Land, they were attacked by the Amalekites, a godless people descended from Esau.

> So Joshua fought the Amalekites as Moses had ordered, and Moses, Aaron and Hur went to the top of the hill. As long as Moses held up his hands, the Israelites were winning, but whenever he lowered his hands, the Amalekites were winning. When Moses' hands grew tired, they took a stone and

> put it under him and he sat on it. Aaron and Hur held his hands up—one on one side, one on the other—so that his hands remained steady till sunset. So Joshua overcame the Amalekite army with the sword....
>
> Moses built an altar and called it The LORD is my Banner [Yahweh Nissi]. (Exodus 17:10–13, 15)

Ann Spangler explains: "Unlike fabric flags, ancient banners were usually made out of wood or metal and shaped into various figures or emblems that could be fastened to a bare staff or a long pole.... A banner carried at the head of an army or planted on a high hill served as a rallying point for troops before battle or as an announcement of a victory already won."[29]

The banner was a symbol of victory! It still is today. Consider the words to America's national anthem, "The Star-Spangled Banner":

> O say, can you see by the dawn's early light,
> What so proudly we hailed at the twilight's last gleaming,
> Whose broad stripes and bright stars through the perilous fight,
> O'er the ramparts we watched, were so gallantly streaming?
> And the rockets' red glare, the bombs bursting in air,
> Gave proof through the night that our flag was still there;
> O say, does that star-spangled banner yet wave,
> O'er the land of the free and the home of the brave?

Chills. Tears. A grateful heart. I am always overcome with gratitude when I sing those words. And I think the same stirring moved in Moses's heart when he called God by the name Yahweh Nissi. God is my victory! God is my banner!

This is the only time in Scripture that the Lord is referred to as our Banner, but it was not the only time God won the victory for His people. Time and time again, God fought for His people, and they waved the flag of victory in the face of apparent defeat (Joshua 10:10, 20, 33; 11:8; Judges 11:21; 20:35). He made the waters rise, the walls fall, and the sun stand still. Yes, God fought for His people and, friend, He will do the same for me and for you.

I love what David proclaimed when he ran toward the enemy giant, Goliath, who dared taunt the armies of the living God.

> You come against me with sword and spear and javelin, *but I come against you in the name of the LORD Almighty, the God of the armies of Israel,* whom you have defied. This day the LORD will hand you over to me, and I'll strike you down and cut off your head. Today I will give the carcasses of the Philistine army to the birds of the air and the beasts of the earth, and the whole world will know that there is a God in Israel. All those gathered here will know that it is not by sword or spear that the LORD saves; for the battle is the LORD's, and he will give all of you into our hands. (1 Samuel 17:45–47)

Now there's a boy who knew Yahweh Nissi. He waved the banner of victory before he even threw the stone. Oh, that we would do the same!

I love what Moses told the Israelites when they realized that the Egyptians were chasing after them.

> Do not be afraid. Stand firm and you will see the deliverance the LORD will bring you today. The Egyptians you see today you will never see again. The LORD will fight for you; you need only to be still. (Exodus 14:13–14)

No child of God needs to live in bondage to feelings of inferiority, insecurity, or inadequacy. No matter what battle you face, God is your victory. No matter what enemy you meet, God is your victory. No matter what struggle you encounter, God is your victory. "But thanks be to God! He gives us the victory through our Lord Jesus Christ" (1 Corinthians 15:57). The Lord is my Banner.

So raise high the banner! Victory is yours.

Let's Pray

Lord, forgive me for acting as if I have to conquer the battles of life on my own. I am embracing the truth that I am a chosen, holy, dearly loved child of the King, who is empowered by God, equipped by the Holy Spirit, and enveloped in Jesus Christ. I can do all things through Him who gives me strength, and I am more than a conqueror through Christ Jesus. In Jesus's name, amen.

Day 4

The Lord Our Peace
Yahweh Shalom

Mary Southerland

Today's Truth

So Gideon built an altar to the LORD there and called it The LORD is Peace [Yahweh Shalom]. (Judges 6:24)

Friend to Friend

Since the sin of Adam and Eve, man's deepest need has been peace with God. We search for peace with a fierce desperation, but our search often leads us to all the wrong places. Some people look for peace in a bottle of prescription pills or alcohol. Others think success, wealth, or the approval of man will bring peace. It won't.

The answer to our need is surprisingly simple: God is our Peace. We will find the rest our hearts long for in a personal relationship with God, who is Yahweh Shalom, the Lord our Peace.

God reveals Himself to us as Yahweh Shalom when we are in over our heads, when He's given us a task that is more than we can handle. The first time God revealed Himself as Yahweh Shalom was when the angel of the Lord appeared to Gideon in Judges 6. Gideon had so many reasons *not* to have peace, including the reality that Israel had been defeated. The fact that Gideon was threshing wheat in a winepress reflected both his small harvest and his fear of being discovered by his enemies, the Midianites. Wheat usually was threshed in an open area by oxen pulling threshing sledges over the stalks, not in a winepress.

But God wanted to lead His people into victory, and Gideon was His chosen instrument. Go figure! If I were assembling a winning team, I would choose the brightest and the best, the most talented, and certainly the most likely people to accomplish my mission. And God chose Gideon? Gideon was the youngest member, the baby—what some might even call the runt—of a small and obscure family. His credentials were unimpressive, to say the least, which is why Gideon felt completely incompetent. Honestly, he had every human right to feel that way. The only thing Gideon did not figure in was the plan of God and the power behind that plan.

Gideon used his weaknesses as an excuse, complaining to God, "My clan is the weakest...and I am the least" (Judges 6:15). I would probably have said something similar, since the Midianites were basically nothing more than barbarians, terrorists, and known nomadic invaders of great number and formidable strength. Yet God wanted unremarkable Gideon to defeat them and free the Israelites. Gideon's response was typical of our own when God calls us to do something that makes little sense and seems impossible.

God's commitment *to* Gideon reaffirmed His presence *with* Gideon and the ease with which Gideon would defeat the Midianites: "The Lord answered, 'I will be with you, and you will strike down all the Midianites together'" (verse 16). The literal translation of *together* is "as if they were but one man." I love it! Here's Gideon, probably the last man anyone would choose to face the Midianites, and God is telling him the victory will be so easy it will seem like he is facing one man instead of an army of fierce invaders. Even then,

Gideon's attitude was lousy. I can almost hear him whining as he blamed God for getting the Israelites into their current mess and voicing major doubts about God's willingness or even His desire to save them. Still, God said Gideon was the man for the job.

When we are honest about our weaknesses, we concede the fact that God alone can accomplish anything good in or through us. God's power is instantly recognizable in obvious weakness. Just as God was with the flawed Gideon, He is with us.

God spoke peace to Gideon's heart when He promised, "Peace! Do not be afraid. You are not going to die" (verse 23). The next verse says that Gideon built an altar and called it "The LORD is Peace." The rest is history. God used Gideon mightily in the days that followed.

Simply knowing the source of peace does not guarantee the presence of peace. We must invite Yahweh Shalom to take up residence in our lives. I can fill my days with so many tasks that peace disintegrates before noon. In Colossians 3:15, Paul encourages us to "let the peace of Christ rule" in our hearts. In the original Greek, the word translated "rule" is an athletic term meaning "to preside over [the games]...and to distribute the prizes."[30] Sounds like a typical day in the life of a woman to me!

In the Greek games, judges rejected any contestants who were not qualified, and they disqualified those who broke the rules. Today, we would call them umpires, and the playing field of peace would be our hearts. "Heart" refers to "the center of one's being." Peace begins its reign in the center of our being, then as we allow it to rule, it works its way into every nook and cranny of life.

I love the story of the little girl who was working on her homework one night. As the hours went by, her parents became curious and asked what she was doing. "I'm writing a report on the condition of the world and how to bring peace," she replied.

Of course, the parents were impressed. "Isn't that a big assignment for just one person?" her dad asked.

With complete confidence, the little girl responded, "Don't worry, Dad. There are three of us working on it." Wouldn't it be wonderful if finding and experiencing peace was that easy?

We work hard at pursuing peace—in our world, our homes, our relationships, and our hearts. Yet, so many of us struggle to actually experience or even understand true peace. It occurs to me that in order to understand what peace *is,* we must first understand what it *is not.*

God's peace is not the absence of conflicts, trials, or difficulties, and it has nothing to do with human beings or human circumstances. In fact, the true peace of God cannot be produced on a human level at all. Any peace that can be conjured by man is fragile, easily destroyed by the storms of life. I don't know about you, but these storms seem to sweep through my life on a regular basis. If we rely on this fallen world for peace, we will forever be disappointed because God alone is the only source of peace. And He made a way for us to know and experience that peace through a personal relationship with His Son, Jesus Christ.

Notice that Paul wrote in Romans 5:1, "We have peace with God through our Lord Jesus Christ." We like to claim the first part of that verse and ignore the vital truth that peace is the result of Jesus reigning in our lives as "Lord of all." Listen, girlfriend, if He is not Lord *of* all, He is not Lord *at* all. And if He is not Lord, then there can be no peace.

The apostle Paul also said it this way: "And the peace of God, which transcends all understanding, will guard your hearts and your minds in Christ Jesus" (Philippians 4:7). As you face the storms of life, face them with God at your side, knowing He is Lord of the rocking boat and keeper of the waves. He rides upon the storm clouds of life, flinging peace into the tempest-filled heart. He is the Lord our Peace. When we know our God as Yahweh Shalom, we will know peace.

Let's Pray

Father God, my heart is filled with chaos and confusion. I feel like I am drowning in my circumstances. My heart is filled with fear. I need the strength and peace that only You can give. Right now, I choose to rest in You. In Jesus's name, amen.

The Lord Is My Shepherd

Yahweh Rohi

Mary Southerland

Today's Truth

The Lord is my shepherd, I shall not be in want. He makes me lie down in green pastures, he leads me beside quiet waters, he restores my soul. He guides me in paths of righteousness for his name's sake. Even though I walk through the valley of the shadow of death, I will fear no evil, for you are with me; your rod and your staff, they comfort me. (Psalm 23:1–4)

Friend to Friend

As a child, I really did have a little lamb whose fleece was white as snow. I can remember the day my mother showed me the lamb and explained that she did not have a bottle with which to feed it. I did. I agreed to give the lamb my bottle if I could have the lamb. I have been fascinated by the unique relationship between sheep and their shepherd ever since.

Shepherding was one of the oldest callings in Israel, even before farming. Shepherds traveled from place to place, living in tents while driving their flocks from one pasture to another, finding places for them to eat and drink, providing shelter from the storms and protection from the heat. Sheep had to eat the right amount of the right kinds of grass at the right times, or they would die. If the sheep ate too little one day and too much the next day, some of the bacteria that lived in the stomach of the sheep created toxins, causing sudden death. The shepherd carefully planned the path and led the way so the sheep had neither too little nor too much grass and water.

Pastures were often lost to extreme heat, which meant the shepherd had to scour the countryside in search of green grass. The sheep and their shepherd lived together every minute of every day. In fact, they were so intimately bound together that individual sheep, even when mixed with other flocks, could recognize the voice of their shepherd and immediately came when called by name.

A shepherd marked the sheep he owned. In fact, for thousands of years, shepherds would notch the ears of their sheep with a sharp knife. Each shepherd had his own distinctive notch that indicated identity and ownership.

Several flocks of sheep gathered together at close of day so shepherds could share the watches of the night, protecting the sheep from wild animals and thieves. Good shepherds would willingly risk their lives to save their flocks from any harm and any enemy.

The needs of sheep, compared to the needs of other animals, are greater because of their instinct to be afraid and, when faced with fearful situations, to run. Sheep can never be left alone. They often stray, requiring the shepherd to find and rescue them.

I definitely fit the profile of a sheep. I grew up in a Christian home, attending church every time the doors were open. I sang all the right songs, spoke all the right words, and did all the right things in front of all the right people. I fervently prayed that my works would validate my faith, and I desperately hoped that by following the rules, I would please the ruler. It wasn't until middle school that the authentic life and spiritual integrity of a dynamic youth pastor made me hunger and thirst for something more. I wanted to know God, not only as my Lord and King but as my Shepherd, the one who would lead me, provide for me, and love me like no other.

During a Saturday evening revival service at our small country church, I sat in my usual spot, clutching the back of the pew in front of me while wrestling with God over the condition of my soul and my eternal security. I was an active church member, a soloist and pianist for our worship services, and even directed a children's choir. I never missed church unless I was deathly ill. I was a leader in our youth group and often brought friends who were lost and needed to know God. I was deeply embarrassed by the thought of walking down that aisle, admitting to everyone that I was a fraud and had been living a lie. I clung to that pew in sheer arrogance and argued that I *was* a Christian. I must be, right? Look at all the good things I had done. I looked like a believer, talked like a believer, and even acted as if I were fully devoted to God.

Then a startling certainty hit me: I knew all *about* God, but I didn't know *Him*. It wasn't enough for me or for God. God's perfect love settles for nothing less than an intimate and loving relationship with each of His children. That night I met God and slowly began to discover who I really am. I am His sheep, in desperate and constant need of a shepherd. Not just any shepherd. I need Yahweh Rohi, the Lord My Shepherd.

I can't count the number of times I have stubbornly stuck to my plan, certain it was better than His, only to end up in a pit somewhere, frantically crying out for help. Fear has driven me to places where I was trapped by doubts and darkness until He rescued me. I often satisfy my hunger by eating the wrong things from the wrong hands found in the wrong places at the wrong times. The result is always the same: my soul soon becomes ravenous for what is good, because I have been stuffing it with what is bad. Yep! I am such a sheep!

Being a sheep can be frightening, but it can also be a good thing. When I am afraid, Yahweh Rohi brings peace. When my heart is broken, Yahweh Rohi comforts me. Even when I found myself in a deep pit of clinical depression, God led me from the darkness into the light. I began to understand the incredible truth that God has planned my very existence in response to His love for me. He has even made provision for the payment of my past, present, and future sin. I am wanted, chosen, and marked for God. I no longer have to live life on my own, because I have a Shepherd. God's love precedes me, goes before me, and surrounds me as I live each day.

The certainty that we are loved fosters peace and eliminates stress. Sheep don't come across as stressed-out creatures. In fact, they seem almost oblivious to danger. Sheep don't worry about where their next meal is coming from, if they will have a place to sleep each night, when the next enemy or thief will attack, or even what the next day holds. When sheep are sick or in need, they simply turn to their shepherd, instinctively knowing he or she will take care of and comfort them.

Knowing we are protected also fosters peace and eliminates stress. Jesus tells us that a shepherd will lay down his life for his sheep (John 10:11). He will fight for them! He does more than prod and pull back with that staff of his. He chases wolves, beats back bears, and double-dares anyone to harm one of his precious lambs.

When we truly recognize God as our Shepherd and begin the journey of becoming His fully devoted followers, we are redeemed by

His forgiveness, made whole by His grace, and marked with His love through the presence and power of the Holy Spirit. We need to remember and often revisit the fact that we are all sheep and that God is our Shepherd, our Yahweh Rohi.

Let's Pray

Thank You, Father, for being so faithful, even when my faith is small and my strength is gone. Help me learn how to trust You more and turn to You first when I am in trouble. I surrender my fears to You, God. I need Your love and guidance to get me through each day. I need Your protection from people and circumstances that are harmful. You are my source, my Shepherd, and my deliverer. Help me choose to trust You in a way that brings You glory and honor. In Jesus's name, amen.

Now It's Your Turn

Time for Reflection

- We began this week with a story of a violent Kansas City storm that tested the limitations of a young boy's trust. He was frightened and wanted his papa to "turn down the storm." We can all surely relate to that! When storms crash into our lives, it helps to remember who God is: Migdal-Oz, our Stronghold and Strong Tower. Identify the people or things that you tend to think of and rely upon as sources of security and contentment in your life. Is God the first place you run to for comfort and protection, or is He your last resort?
- Knowing God as your stronghold will increase your willingness to trust Him. Read Proverbs 3:5–6. What steps are we advised to take in this passage?

  Step 1: Trust in the Lord with all your heart

  Step 2: on your own intelligence rely not

  Step 3: In all your ways be mindful of him

  What reward will you experience when you take these steps?

  Reward: He will make straight your paths

  Which of the three steps do you struggle with the most? Why? Trust
- Identify a recent storm that you've experienced in life. How would you rate your response to this storm: A, B or C?

  Fear the lord and turn away from evil

A. Got soaked (drenched, even. Major fail. Would really love a redo.)

B. Got through (had good moments and bad moments. Worried…then trusted…then worried…then trusted…)

C. Got shielded (thrived in the strength, peace, and joy of the Lord! Not perfectly, but purposefully. All glory to *His* powerful name!)

What changes, if any, do you need to make in order to answer C in the future?

God is El Sali, our Strength. Read the first half of Psalm 84:5: "Blessed are those whose strength is in you." To whom is this comment directed? In what ways has this proved true in your life?

Scripture links hope and strength together. Read Isaiah 40:29–31: "He [the LORD] gives strength to the weary and increases the power of the weak. Even youths grow tired and weary, and young men stumble and fall; but those who hope in the LORD will renew their strength. They will soar on wings like eagles; they will run and not grow weary, they will walk and not be faint."

In the movie *The Wizard of Oz,* the Wicked Witch tried to keep Dorothy from her hope. What is or has been a barrier to your hope?

Like Dorothy, are you facing any scary struggles or frustrating setbacks? Discuss.

Nehemiah 8:10 says, "The joy of the LORD is your strength." What do you think the joy of the Lord looks like? Have you seen it lately? If so, in whom, and how did you recognize it?

- On a scale of 1–10, how often do you display the joy of the Lord as your strength? (1 = Never, 10 = Always) ______

  How often would you like to experience and show it?

  ____

  What would it take to get you to that frequency?

  ____

  Are you willing to do that? YES or NO (circle one)

  Why or why not? ______________________________

  ____

- When feelings of insecurity, inferiority, and inadequacy render us far from the God-confident women we long to be, Yahweh Nissi, the LORD is my Banner, will fight for us and give us strength for each battle, just as He did for Moses and the Israelites. Read Exodus 14:13–14: "Do not be afraid. Stand firm and you will see the deliverance the LORD will bring you today. The Egyptians you see today you will never see again. The LORD will fight for you; you need only to be still."

  How will you let these verses shape your perspective today?

- God is also Yahweh Shalom (the Lord is Peace) and Yahweh Rohi (the Lord My Shepherd). Read Psalm 23:1–6. Beside each declaration, write the words of the psalm that substantiate the statement listed. We have given a few examples to help you get started.

  God will meet my every need. "I shall not be in want."

  God gives me rest. "He leads me beside quiet waters."

  God's presence brings restoration. you restore my strength

  God gives my life purpose. guide me along the right path

God comforts me. ______________________________

____

God will never leave me. ______________________________

____

God deals with my enemies. ______________________________

____

I will worship Him forever. ______________________________

____

Now summarize the benefits of allowing the Lord to be your Peace and your Shepherd.

____

____

____

____

Wrap up your response time with prayer. Move from confession, to adoration, to thanksgiving, and end with your petitions (personal prayer needs).

Going Deeper with God

List: the names of God and their meanings that were covered in the devotions this week.

1. ______________________________
2. ______________________________
3. ______________________________
4. ______________________________
5. ______________________________

Read and **contemplate:** Psalm 23.

Reflect and respond: On the lines below, list a few of the storms you are currently facing.

Cancer re-currance
Mother-elderly - lonely
Megan- Paris

Surrender each one to God, asking Him to fill its place with His peace. Now, walk in that peace. When the waves come, remember that the storm now belongs to your Father.

Your GiG *Knowing God by Name* Journal

Spend a few moments contemplating and journaling about some of the scriptural truths that moved your heart as you read the devotions this week. Then use the space below to collect your thoughts or write a prayer of response to God.

4-7-16

Jo Ann Hood
Jag Threadgill - RSV
Lauren McPherson - 5yr. old cancer
Sean - Betty's grandson
Julie Fisher-Jenny Mayo's sister - pregnant

The LORD is a refuge for the oppressed, a stronghold in times of trouble. Those who know your name will trust in you, for you, LORD, have never forsaken those who seek you. (Psalm 9:9–10)

Day 1

My Savior and My Deliverer
Ysuah

Sharon Jaynes

Today's Truth

Guide me in your truth and teach me, for you are God my Savior, and my hope is in you all day long. (Psalm 25:5)

Friend to Friend

Some years ago, I was excited to visit the San Francisco Bay Area for our family vacation. My heart's desire and prayer for each day was that we would see God's handiwork in creation and be reminded of His greatness.

When my husband, son, and I arrived, we plotted our course and then took off like three eager explorers. First we traveled south along the rugged shoreline and marveled at the two-hundred-foot regal cliffs that pushed heavenward with waves splashing at their feet. Then we traveled north and drank in the beauty of acres and acres of neatly pruned vineyards aligned on grassy rolling hills in the Napa Valley wine country. We hiked through the majestic redwood forest, dwarfed by thousand-year-old, 260-foot giants. Ah, I was loving God's creation.

You can imagine my dismay when the "boys" wanted to go to Alcatraz, an old rock prison in the middle of the San Francisco Bay, just a mile and a quarter from the shore. Not my idea of a good time, and not my idea of "enjoying God's creation." From 1934 to 1963, Alcatraz—also known as the Devil's Island of America and the Rock—housed the country's most corrupt, incorrigible criminals. Al Capone and Machine Gun Kelly were just two of its more notorious residents.

There is no road to the prison, so we took a ferry across the bay. As we taxied up to the Rock and stared at the shell of concrete walls, barbed wire, and iron bars, an eerie feeling crept over my body. We each picked up headphones and a recorder and toured the prison while listening to the taped voices of various prisoners recounting their days behind bars. I walked into a cell called the hole, closed my eyes, and tried to imagine solitary confinement with no light, no sound, and no voice but my own. My heart grew heavy as I thought about the souls who had passed through those musty halls...souls filled with darkness, depression, and despair.

But as I rounded the final corner of the tour, I saw an amazing sight: a white-haired eighty-year-old grandfather with crystal-blue, laughing eyes and a radiant smile spread across his wrinkled face. A line formed as tourists stood waiting for him to sign his name and number on his autobiography, *Alcatraz from Inside.* This precious man before me was Jim Quillen, ex-prisoner #AZ586. He had spent ten years of his life, from 1942 to 1952, behind bars in this prison built to house the most dangerous criminals of his day. I looked into his eyes as we spoke. This was not the face of a dangerous man. What had happened to change his life?

I didn't have to flip many pages in his book to find the answer. In it he wrote, "It was only through the grace of our Lord Jesus Christ and His intercession, that my life of hopeless incarceration was averted. His help and forgiveness permitted me to obtain freedom, family, and a useful and productive place in society."[31]

That explained everything.

You and I are not much different from Mr. Quillen. While he had been a prisoner in Alcatraz, you and I have been prisoners to sin. No, most of us weren't shackled with chains, locked behind bars, or separated from the rest of the world. But we all were prisoners shackled by shame, locked behind guilt, and separated from God. We were on death row with no hope of parole. But God…

Paul reminds us that "all have sinned and fall short of the glory of God" (Romans 3:23). No one has ever been good enough to get out of the jail of condemnation by their merits. The penalty for that sin is the death sentence and eternal separation from God…hell (Romans 6:23). However—oh, this is so good!—"God demonstrates his own love for us in this: While we were still sinners, Christ died for us" (Romans 5:8). Jesus went before the Judge of all creation and offered to pay the penalty for your sin. He knew the cost. He understood the pain. And yet He gave His life to set you free.

Salvation is not something that you or I could earn for ourselves or do for ourselves. As David said of the Lord, "You are God my Savior" (Psalm 25:5). He also wrote,

> The Lord is my rock, my fortress and my deliverer;
> my God is my rock, in whom I take refuge,
> my shield and the horn of my salvation.
> He is my stronghold, my refuge and my savior.
> (2 Samuel 22:2–3)

God is the only One who *can* save us. Paul wrote to the Ephesians, "For it is by grace you have been saved, through faith—and this not from yourselves, it is the gift of God" (Ephesians 2:8). Salvation is a gift. It is received by faith, and even the faith to receive it is a gift from God.

But you have to decide whether or not you'll accept this gift. Jesus will not force anyone to step out of sin's prison and breathe the air of freedom. The Bible tells us, "For God so loved the world that he gave his one and only Son, that whoever *believes* in him shall not perish but have eternal life" (John 3:16). It also says "that if you *confess* with your mouth, 'Jesus is Lord,' and *believe* in your heart that God raised him from the dead, you will be saved. For it is with your heart that you *believe* and are justified, and it is with your mouth that you confess and are *saved*" (Romans 10:9–10).

The word *saved* has been tossed about so much in the church that I fear it has lost its wonder and mystery. So what does it mean to be saved?

In the original Greek, the word *salvation* is used five times in Romans, and the verb form, *saved,* occurs eight times. Both terms suggest "deliverance" or "rescue." So what are we rescued from? Through Jesus Christ we are saved from lostness (Luke 19:10), the wrath of God (Romans 5:9), the penalty of sin (Romans 8:1), the realm of darkness (Colossians 1:13), eternal separation from God (Ephesians 2:13), and eternal punishment in hell (Revelation 20:14–15). Salvation is more than a "get out of jail free" card. It is more than a ticket into heaven. We *are saved* from the penalty of sin the moment we believe. We *are being saved* from the power of sin as we continue to live on this earth and become more and more conformed to the image of Christ. And we *will be saved* from the presence of sin when we leave this earthly body to spend eternity with God.

All this is ours when we accept God's gift through faith (Romans 3:22). We are not saved by how we behave but by how we believe. Saving faith involves our entire being: mind, will, and emotions. With the mind we understand the truth of the gospel, with the will we choose to submit to God and make Jesus Lord of our lives, and with the emotions we express sorrow over our sin and joy over God's mercy and grace.

Eternal life begins the moment you believe. God's desire is for you to experience the abundant life here on earth (John 10:10). It is passing from spiritual death to spiritual life in the twinkling of an eye (John 3:3). When you embrace Jesus as your Lord and Savior, you walk *out of* the jail cell of shame and condemnation and *into* the kingdom of Christ. You become a brand-new creation (2 Corinthians 5:17) with a clean slate (Psalm 103:12). "If the Son sets you free, you will be free indeed" (John 8:36). "There is therefore now no condemnation for those who are in Christ Jesus. For the law of the Spirit of life has set you free in Christ Jesus from the law of sin and death" (Romans 8:1–2, ESV).

Now that is good news. That is the gospel.

I went back over to Mr. Quillen, sat by his side, and chatted for a few moments as he autographed my copy of his book. Then God spoke to my heart, *You prayed that you would see My handiwork on this trip to San Francisco and be reminded of My greatness. This man is some of my best work.*

In just a few short days, I was reminded of God's unchanging strength by the majestic rock cliffs of the shoreline and of His nurturing care as the Vinedresser in the hills of the wine country. I saw a picture of God's protective canopy over His children in the towering redwoods of the forest. But when I looked into Jim Quillen's eyes, I saw God's most incredible masterpiece: a changed life...a soul set free.

Let's Pray

Lord, thank You for setting me free. Thank You for sending Jesus to pay the penalty for my sin so that I could walk out of the dark prison of sin and into the radiant freedom of Christ. Thank You for being my deliverer, my Savior who set me free. In Jesus's name, amen.

If you can't remember a time when you accepted Jesus as your Savior and Lord, now is the perfect time to do so. If you would like to accept God's precious gift of freedom, pray the following from your heart:

Dear heavenly Father, I come to You today as a sinner in need of a Savior. I confess that I have sinned and made many mistakes. I am unable to live a holy life on my own. I repent of my sin; I'm turning away from my sinful life and running toward You. I believe in my heart that Jesus Christ is Your Son, who was born of a virgin, lived a perfect life, and gave Himself as a sacrifice to pay the penalty for my sins. I believe that He rose from the dead on the third day and now lives forever with You. I come to You in faith, believing, and thank You for giving me the gift of eternal life. In Jesus's name, amen.

God of Forgiveness
Yahweh Hesed

Mary Southerland

Today's Truth

But You are a God of forgiveness, gracious and compassionate, slow to anger and abounding in lovingkindness. (Nehemiah 9:17, NASB)

Friend to Friend

Our air conditioner was just not getting the job done. It only partially cooled the house, running night and day, doubling our already exorbitant electric bill. I called John, our friendly air-conditioning repairman, with a desperate plea for help. When he came to the house, the first thing he did was remove the filter from the vent. It was filthy, completely covered by some nasty gray gunk! Changing the air filter had never been one of my top priorities, as evidenced by the dirt- and hair-caked object in front of me.

With a disapproving scowl wrinkling his weathered face, John continued working, muttering under his breath. I pretended not to hear. Eventually he removed the coil, thrust it in front of me, pointed at the almost unrecognizable object, and with a sigh of exasperation asked, "What is this?"

"John," I responded, "how am I supposed to know what that is? You're the air-conditioning expert."

He did not find my comment funny.

To avoid his scathing glare, I stepped forward to closely examine the obviously faulty coil. It was covered with layers of dog hair, compliments of our West Highland terrier and Australian cattle dog; cat hair, compliments of Sassy, Chocolate, and Tiger; and dust, compliments of me!

John then chastised me for not changing the filter more often. He ended his discourse with an ominous explanation. "Mrs. Southerland, this unit was never meant to work under this kind of load. It's working as hard as it can, but it's not strong enough to do something it was never intended to do." John then replaced the air filter, cleaned out the coil along with our bank account, and left the scene of the crime. The electric bill went back down, the house was cooler than it had been in months, and the unit worked like it was supposed to work.

That experience with our malfunctioning air conditioner illustrates a vital spiritual truth: left unaddressed, sin clogs up our souls with a load we are not designed to operate under. I was not created to bear the burden of my sin nor does God expect me to do so. He already paid for my sin and only one payment is required. The same is true for you, girlfriend.

God's forgiveness, grace, and love permeate Scripture from beginning to end. Eve may have been the first sinner, but she was also the first one to experience the loving forgiveness of God. And at the end of time, on that day when we stand before God, clothed in the blood and forgiveness of Jesus, we will say with the prophet Micah, "Who is a God like you, who pardons sin and forgives the transgression of the remnant of his inheritance? You do not stay angry forever but delight to show mercy" (Micah 7:18).

The Hebrew language has a word for this lifelong love that is richer and deeper than English has ever conceived of: *hesed* (HEH-sed). Based in a covenantal relationship, hesed expresses a steadfast, rock-solid faithfulness that endures throughout eternity. Isaiah 54:10 describes this love beautifully: "Though the mountains be shaken and the hills be removed, yet my unfailing love [*hesed*] for you will not be shaken."

We are saved by God's hesed, and nothing we do or don't do will ever be good enough to earn the love of God or the forgiveness that His love offers. The apostle Paul tells us that salvation is a gift—period: "For it is by grace you have been saved, through faith—and this not from yourselves, it is the gift of God" (Ephesians 2:8). If we could earn salvation, we'd be simply receiving wages for works we have done all on our own. But we can't achieve forgiveness through our own efforts; we are saved through faith in God alone: "He [God] is so rich in kindness and grace that he purchased our freedom with the blood of his Son and forgave our sins" (Ephesians 1:7, NLT).

Salvation and the blessings of God are His gifts to us. Our role is to receive them. But sometimes it seems we take these gifts far too lightly, forgetting their true cost. God is the source of all forgiveness. The tangible reality of His forgiveness is seen in the life, death, burial, and resurrection of His Son, Jesus Christ.

Several years ago an interesting cartoon appeared in the *Saturday Review of Literature.* Little George Washington is standing with an ax in his hand. In front of him, lying on the ground, is the famous cherry tree. He has already made his smug admission that he did it because, after all, he "cannot tell a lie." However, his frustrated father is standing beside him saying, "All right, so you admit it! You *always* admit it! The question is when are you going to stop *doing* it?"

That is the question at hand, girlfriend. How often do we soothe our bothered conscience with admissions of sin, presenting them to the Father as obedience to the biblical directive to confess our sin? True confession, however, goes a step further and results in a change in lifestyle and behavior. This step is called repentance.

I once associated the command to repent with old-fashioned gospel meetings and screaming preachers on television. In reality, repentance is the cornerstone of genuine forgiveness and gives credibility to the very act of confessing sin. To *repent* simply means to "turn away from." When we choose to turn from our sin and turn to God and His ways, we are practicing true repentance—which brings us back into relationship with the God of forgiveness, who stands ready to clean the gunk of sin out of our souls. "Then if my people who are called by my name will humble themselves and pray and seek my face and turn from their wicked ways, I will hear from heaven and will forgive their sins and restore their land" (2 Chronicles 7:14, NLT).

What does it look like when we truly repent? The sinful woman in Luke 7 offers us a beautiful portrait of genuine repentance: "As she stood behind him at his feet weeping, she began to wet his feet with her tears. Then she wiped them with her hair, kissed them and poured perfume on them" (verse 38).

Notice that this woman stood *behind* Jesus, like a caught child too ashamed to look her father in the eyes. Standing so close to Jesus transformed her, and she began to weep. Jesus was as pure as she was sinful. Every ugly thought, word, or deed of her past must have flooded her heart and shattered it. And then, the most amazing miracle of all happened. God, the One who forgives, worked through

His Son to heal every wounded part of this woman's heart and expose and forgive every sin she had ever committed. Only God can do that.

Standing in His presence, she somehow knew He understood everything she could not say and loved her in spite of her sin. Tears of sorrow and joy spilled down the face of this sinful woman onto the feet of the One who truly loved her. Those tears may well have been the first authentic prayer of her life. I believe she was oblivious to those watching as she dropped to her knees and began kissing the feet of Jesus while pouring perfume over them.

The Greek word translated in these verses as "kissed" literally means "to kiss again and again." She then dropped to her knees, let down her hair as a sign of total submission, and used it to dry the feet of Jesus. The social custom of the day demanded that women keep their hair bound up. To let it down was considered a brazen act and could even be grounds for divorce, but this woman was beyond caring about social customs and earthly rules. She was desperate and conducting eternal business. She'd found what she had been searching for in every wrong relationship, every failure, and every dead-end choice. She'd found God, the forgiver, at work through His Son, Jesus Christ. If we want to experience true forgiveness, we must experience God, and that can only be accomplished through first knowing Jesus.

It is important to notice that Jesus did not move away from her. He didn't stop her or condemn her. He knew exactly why she was there, and He was thrilled! He saw her heart and received her humble action as an acceptable gift of worship.

Jesus looked past her sin and saw her heart crying out for forgiveness. Notice His response in verse 48: "Your sins are forgiven." Wow! God always majors in unconditional love, amazing grace, and total forgiveness. The tense of the Greek verb translated as "forgiven" indicates this forgiveness of sin was completed in the past, continues through the present, and will keep working in the future. The forgiveness of God is complete and eternal. Forgiveness begins and ends with God.

Powerful living flows from a heart that has repented of every known sin and received the gift of forgiveness that God so freely offers. Turn to Him today and celebrate His love and His forgiveness. Celebrate your God who forgives!

Let's Pray

Father God, I come to You today, seeking forgiveness. I have sinned. I choose now to turn from that sin and obey You. Please search my heart and life. Reveal every wrong attitude and action that is keeping me from knowing and truly worshiping You. Father, I am tired of trying to live life on my own. I am desperate for You. Right now, I surrender everything I am and ever hope to be to You. In Jesus's name, amen.

My Redeemer
Haggo'el

Gwen Smith

Today's Truth

For I know that my Redeemer lives. (Job 19:25, ESV)

Friend to Friend

A crisp chill slipped through the window as I headed to the couch to get with God before rushing into my day. I filled my mug with coffee, lit a cinnamon-bun-scented jar candle, and settled into my corner spot. Before I could get comfortable, however, I realized that the combination of the morning breeze and the ceiling fan made the room a bit nippy for my shorts-clad legs. I jumped up from the couch and turned the ceiling fan off—for possibly the first time in five or six months.

As I nestled back down into my comfy prayer corner, I looked up at the fan, now still, and drew a deep breath of surprise. Dirt! All over the blades of my ceiling fan! And when I say that I saw dirt, let me tell you, it wasn't just a smidgeon; it was a thick carpeting of grime. *Yuck.* When did that happen? How did it get there? Note to self: *clean fan today.*

I brought my Bible and prayer journal to my lap, ready to talk to God and seek His direction for the day. But before I could even lift my pen and open the Word, I heard the Spirit whisper to my soul, *Be still.*

"I'm here, Lord! Ready to talk. Ready to pray," my heart responded.

Again, the whisper, *Be still.*

"Like the fan, Lord?" I wondered.

Then it hit me: when I still my soul to listen quietly, God gently shows me the dirt on the blades of my heart. You see, I'm an action girl. I love to move and chat and go, go, go. Dust does not settle on my days, but—as God reminded me that morning—dirt sure can settle on my heart.

I nodded knowingly. "It's Your kindness that leads me to repentance, oh, Lord" (Romans 2:4).

When I slow to still and know that He is God, holiness looks straight in the eyes of my heart. In light of His holiness, my wretchedness is revealed. His love and kindness reveal my spiritual disarray and cause my heart to ache for restoration. So I confess. I confess my mess and ask Him to sweep away my heart dirt. And His mercy runs to me. Before the confessions leave my tongue, the blades of my heart are sparkling. Wiped clean with the righteousness of beautiful, far-reaching grace.

God's redemptive grace can wipe *any* heart-blade clean.

In the beginning, at the very moment that rebellion collided with perfection and invaded the hearts of humanity, God set in motion a plan of redemption. His plan was Jesus, His only Son, who came to redeem us, to save us, to wash us clean from sin. He is an awesome Redeemer, One who gives beauty for ashes, comfort for mourning, and freedom to the shackled. A Savior who imputes His righteousness to the wretched, shines light in the darkest places, and breathes hope into the weariest of souls.

Scripture introduces us to a guy who experienced God's redemption in beautifully deep ways. Job was a good man. I mean a *really* good man. The Bible says, "This man was blameless and upright; he feared God and shunned evil" (Job 1:1). He lived life the right way. He honored God, loved his family, and was both faithful and patient. *Good man.*

You'd think such a standout guy would pretty much have a cake life, right? So *not* right. Let me just say this: good-guy Job went through some stuff. Boy, did he go through some stuff. We're talking major big-league stuff. He *had* it all and then *lost* it all: his children, his wealth, and his health. Gone. In a blink.

Don't just skim over that last paragraph.

This man lost his children, for goodness' sake!

They died.

All ten of them. At the same time.

I can't even fathom the thought of losing one of my children, let alone all of my children. *Shiver.* Job knew brokenness on levels that few of us will ever come close to experiencing. He knew ashes. He knew mourning. He knew darkness. He knew weary.

On the front end of the pain, he demonstrated faith. Big faith. He held on to his integrity, accepted his circumstances, and blessed the name of the Lord in spite of the horror he endured. And he worshiped! Can you believe he worshiped?

> Then he fell to the ground in worship and said:
> "Naked I came from my mother's womb,
>   and naked I will depart.
> The LORD gave and the LORD has taken away;

may the name of the LORD be praised."

In all this, Job did not sin by charging God with wrongdoing. (Job 1:20–22)

Job went through loss after loss, test after test, and friend-with-bad-advice after friend-with-bad-advice who spoke condemnation instead of comfort. All that and his wife wanted him to "curse God and die!" (2:9). *Nice.* Isn't it amazing how some people can say dumb things that completely misrepresent the heart of God in times of struggle? Oh, friend, let us be women who are quick to comfort and slow to speak advice.

Stepping down from my soapbox…

When his suffering continued even after his faithful response, Job was in anguish (6:2; 7:11). *Understandable!* He wanted to die because the pain was so unrelenting (6:8–10). He called out to God and asked Him to reveal where he had gone wrong. Then he repented of the sins he knew he had committed.

Job lamented. Stomped his feet a bit. Got a smidge sassy and frustrated with God. And he wondered if God even cared. Then God answered his complaints, corrected his heart, and set the wheels in motion for one of the most amazing shows of redemption the world has ever seen.

In time, God shined light into Job's darkness, spoke gladness to his mourning, and brought beauty to his ashes. He redeemed Job's life from the dark pit of brokenness. Through it all, Job humbly and wholeheartedly worshiped the Lord. Not perfectly, but persistently. Job, who was the first in Scripture to ever call God his Redeemer, did not wait until his suffering had passed. He worshiped God as his Redeemer in the midst of his trials—by faith. Faith that proved well placed. Even though he longed for evidence that God cared, Job clung to the certainty that God was his Redeemer when, in a time of prolonged agony, he confidently called Him Haggo'el. "For I know that my Redeemer lives" (19:25, ESV).

Haggo'el is Hebrew for "God the Redeemer." Another Hebrew term used to describe God as our Redeemer is *Adonai Tsuri v'go'ali,* which means "YHWH (LORD) my Rock and Redeemer," a phrase we find in Psalm 19:14: "Let the words of my mouth and the meditation of my heart be acceptable in your sight, O LORD, my rock and my redeemer" (ESV).[32]

God also names *Himself* our Redeemer in Scripture: "Then you will know that I, the LORD, am your Savior, your Redeemer, the Mighty One of Jacob" (Isaiah 60:16).

You see? God is all about redemption.

His love for humanity runs deeper than the deepest recesses of our depravity. His love extends further than your past, higher than your disappointments, wider than your heart wounds, and deeper than a cavernous pit of depression. God's plan of redemption is for every person, no matter where you've been, no matter what you've been through, no matter what you've done.

But, alas, there's a catch.

There's always a catch, right?

The catch is, your redemption has to be personal.

God desires to extend grace to every one of us, but each of us must accept or reject God's redemption plan by accepting or rejecting His Son, Jesus Christ. Redemption begins and ends with Jesus. "For God loved the world so much that he gave his one and only Son, so that everyone who believes in him will not perish but have eternal life" (John 3:16, NLT).

Redemption is for me.

Redemption is for you.

Do you believe that? Have you made it personal with God?

Whether you are at work, at home, at the hospital, or in a jail cell, He's whispering, *Be still—and let Me clean and restore you.* Whether you are struggling with life strains or are in a season of reprieve. *Be still.* Whether you have a house full of crazy noise or an apartment filled with ordered quiet. *Be still.* Whether the diagnosis is cancer or the sting of betrayal is fresh, whether the hope you cling to resounds or you are weary and unsettled. *Be still.* Know that He is God. Know that He is good. Call out to your Redeemer.

Confess your mess before Him.

Consider His love.

Then in the stillness, respond from your heart.

Let's Pray

Dear Lord, my Redeemer, I'm here. I'm still. Please reveal my heart-dirt. [Pause to listen and reflect.] *I confess these sins to You: ___________________. And I ask that You remove them as far as the east is from the west. Thanks for capturing me with Your grace once again. In Jesus's name I pray, amen.*

The God of Mercy and Grace

Sharon Jaynes

Today's Truth

Blessed be the God and Father of our Lord Jesus Christ, the Father of mercies and God of all comfort, who comforts us in all our affliction so that we will be able to comfort those who are in any affliction with the comfort with which we ourselves are comforted by God. (2 Corinthians 1:3–4, NASB)

Friend to Friend

I've always thought of the parable of the wayward son's return home in Luke 15 as the story of the prodigal son. After all, that's what the heading in my Bible says. But lately I've come to see the story as being much more about the father than the son.

According to Webster's Collegiate Dictionary, *prodigal* doesn't mean "wayward," but rather "recklessly spendthrift." It paints a word picture of someone who spends until there is nothing left to spend, who is recklessly extravagant, and who has spent everything he has. That certainly seems to fit the picture of the prodigal son, but let's look a little closer at his dad, for he was "recklessly extravagant" as well.

The younger son in the parable was a young man who wanted what he wanted when he wanted it. What he *didn't* want was to wait until his father died to receive his inheritance, so he asked for it while his father was still alive. In that culture such a request clearly suggested, "I wish you were already dead."

The father gave his son his inheritance and watched him walk into the sunset to squander it all. The father knew full well what would happen as he watched his son leave with moneybags full and soul empty. Within a few months' time, all the money was gone. The son had spent it on fast women and fast living. He woke up one morning to find himself dirty, destitute, and despairing. "He began to be in need" (verse 14). Oh, how those words stir my heart. For it is when we see that we are in need that the God of Mercy and Grace responds.

In order to stay alive, the son took a job as a farmhand, feeding pigs. Things became so desperate that he even considered quieting his hunger pangs with the pods that the pigs were eating, which was just about as low as a Jewish boy could sink.

After a time, the boy "came to his senses" (verse 17) and realized that his father's servants had better living conditions than he did, so he planned to return and beg forgiveness. He practiced his repentance speech, headed home, and hoped for the best.

And where do we find the father as his son's head appears on the horizon? Waiting. Hoping. Praying. "But while he was still a long way off, his father saw him and was *filled with compassion* for him; he ran to his son, threw his arms around him and kissed him" (verse 20).

I can see the father now. Panning the horizon day after day. Then he catches a glimpse of the familiar shape of a head...a recognizable frame, though slumped. *Could it be? Could it be?* he wonders. With pounding heart and tearing eyes, the father picks up the hem of his garment and runs as fast as his aging legs can muster. And before the son even has a chance to recite his practiced plea for forgiveness, his dad smothers him with kisses, forgives him completely, and welcomes him home unconditionally.

Not only did the father welcome his son home with open arms, but he also threw him a grand party and gave him a new wardrobe to boot. I'd call that lavish. I'd call that "recklessly spendthrift"—a father who gives, holding nothing back. Amazing grace, how sweet the sound. Merciful Father, how lavish the love.

In his letter to the Corinthians, Paul refers to God as the "Father of mercies" (2 Corinthians 1:3, NASB). Another Bible translation of the same verse uses the words "Father of compassion" (NIV). The words *mercy* and *grace* go hand in hand; they are two sides of one holy coin. While *grace* is receiving a blessing we don't deserve, *mercy* is *not* receiving the punishment that we *do* deserve.

We've all made mistakes. We've all sinned (Romans 3:23). The Bible promises that "if we confess our sins, he [the God of Mercy and Grace] is faithful and just and will forgive us our sins and purify us from all unrighteousness" (1 John 1:9). You might know that verse. You might believe that promise. But let me ask you this: Have you received that truth? Have you forgiven yourself? Have you accepted the gift of forgiveness from the God of Mercy and Grace?

There is no sin that is too grave for God's mercy and grace to forgive. No sin you could ever commit is too terrible for God to reach down into the pit, pull you out, and forgive. It is difficult to fathom such extravagantly reckless spendthrift love, but it is a gift from God. He has wrapped up forgiveness as a beautiful gift and written your name on the tag. Many leave His gift unopened because they cannot grasp the idea that God meant it for them—for *their* horrible sin. Many admire the wrapping and marvel at the gift's enormity, but refuse to actually pluck the bow from its lid and receive the freedom of forgiveness...the love gift of mercy and grace.

Ponder these truths for a moment:

> The faithful love of the LORD never ends!
> His mercies never cease.
> Great is his faithfulness;
> his mercies begin afresh each morning. (Lamentations 3:22–23, NLT)

(Every morning, girlfriend. Every morning.)

> But because of his great love for us, God, who is rich in mercy, made us alive with Christ even when we were dead in transgressions—it is by grace you have been saved.... For it is by grace you have been saved, through faith—and this not from yourselves, it is the gift of God. (Ephesians 2:4–5, 8)

> And if by grace, then it is no longer by works; if it were, grace would no longer be grace. (Romans 11:6)

So what are you going to do with God's mercy and grace? Stay in the pigpen of shame, condemnation, and guilt, convinced you've gone too far, fallen too many times, sinned too much? Oh no, friend. You were not made for the pigpen. The greater the sin, the greater the mercy and grace. The God of Mercy and Grace has extended the gift. It's up to you to accept it, open it, believe it, and receive it. "Let us then approach the throne of grace with *confidence,* so that we may receive mercy and find grace to help us in our time of need" (Hebrews 4:16).

Today, sit in the presence of God's lavish love and accept His gift. Amazing grace, how sweet the sound.

Let's Pray

God of Mercy and Grace, I have trotted off like the wayward son so many times. Today, I repent, turn from my sinful tendency toward squandering Your gifts, and turn toward home. I run to You. Thank You for opening Your arms and welcoming me home. Thank You for cleaning off my pigpen filth with the washcloth of Your mercy and grace. In Jesus's name, amen.

Day 5

The Lord My Sanctifier

Yahweh M'Kaddesh

Gwen Smith

Today's Truth

Keep my statutes and do them; I am the Lord who sanctifies you. (Leviticus 20:8, ESV)

Friend to Friend

As Christian believers, we are called to live set-apart lives. To be holy as God is holy (Leviticus 19:2; 1 Thessalonians 4:7). To be in the world, but not of the world. God is the source of all holiness, and in order to live set-apart lives—in other words, to be sanctified—we must spend time with Him and allow His Holy Spirit to fuel us.

God loves us too much to leave us as we are. He wants much more for us than that! God's plan is to make us more like Himself—to sanctify us. He is Yahweh M'Kaddesh, the Lord My Sanctifier. Sanctification is defined as "the process by which the Holy Spirit shapes us into more holy and Christlike people. It's a natural part of a Christian's growth in spiritual maturity."[33]

Reverend Billy Graham said it this way: "Being a Christian is more than just an instantaneous conversion. It is a daily process whereby you grow to be more and more like Christ."[34]

Let's take this street level. I don't know what your days look like, but mine are pretty full. They start early and end late. Once the sun rises, it seems that coffee isn't the only thing brewing in my house. An invisible competition for my time and attention percolates throughout the day. The competitors are often "good things" that end up being "time-robbing things" that keep me from God's best and God's presence. When I'm kept from God's presence, I'm also kept from growing in His divine grace, a major loss for me.

Have you been there?

Does an invisible competition brew in your home and heart too?

I'm thinking: *Yes.* We all struggle with this.

So what are some of these "good things" that end up being "time-robbing distractions"? They look different for each of us. Like snowflakes and fingerprints, all of us are unique—even in our struggles. But certain ones seem to crop up frequently in my conversations with other women: activity overload, electronics, excessive shopping, overcommitment to volunteer work at church or community service. None of these things are bad in and of themselves, but they become a hindrance to sanctification when we allow them to take precedence over our personal growth toward Christlikeness.

A big contender for my attention is electronics. I'm an e-girl. I love my MacBook Pro computer, my iPhone, e-mail, instant messaging, and the World Wide Web. Though I'm admittedly fully immersed in the e-life, I'm also cognizant of the fact that technology has become a dangerous addiction and spiritual deterrent to many.

I struggle with this personally. These electronic forums offer a powerful and efficient opportunity for us to connect with other people 24/7. While much of social media, online surfing, and e-mailing is innocent, encouraging, and fun, these activities also present us with opportunities to sin and to become distracted from set-apart living.

Over the past several years, Facebook, Twitter, Pinterest, blogs, instant messaging, games, and texting have replaced many of our face-to-face conversations. For some of us, time with electronics has diminished our devotion time with the Lord. Online activities have become a continual source of temptation, providing an opportunity to live a fantasy, a momentary escape from the daily grind—or even reasons to be envious of those who have more "friends" or whose posts receive more responses.

A friend of mine recently said, "My computer whispers to me." *Yikes!* Mine does too. I readily admit that all too often I give in to the lure of e-life, responding to yet another audio alert indicating "I've got mail" or to a notification that someone has left me a message on a social media site. As a result, I rob myself of productive time.

We are warned about our use of time in Scripture: "Be very careful, then, how you live—not as unwise but as wise, making the most of every opportunity, because the days are evil" (Ephesians 5:15–16).

Now, hear me clearly on this: I am not saying that electronics or computers are bad. I'm simply suggesting that it would be wise for each of us to prayerfully consider the amount of time and energy we devote to these things.

How can we be set apart in our e-life? How can we establish healthy boundaries that will protect our purity and our time with God? Perhaps we could start by honestly comparing the amount of time we commit to technology and social media versus the amount of time we commit to spending in God's Word and in His presence each day. (Did that sting? Rest assured, it stings me too.)

Maybe you don't share my particular issues with technology. Is there perhaps some other area of your life that demands excessive attention, some distraction that is preventing your deeper spiritual growth?

The good news is that we can turn to God for direction in all of this. Remember? Yahweh M'Kaddesh, our Sanctifier, wants His daughters to continually grow in divine grace. His Word points us to a vital promise of wisdom that will guide us in holiness: "If any of you lacks wisdom, he should ask God, who gives generously to all without finding fault, and it will be given to him" (James 1:5). How awesome is that? God loves us so much that He offers us an endless supply of wisdom. We just need to ask, so that we are enabled to walk in His wisdom and to live each day in His holiness—completely and fully set apart for Him.

The Exhaustive Dictionary of Bible Names sums it up this way:

> The term "holiness" from the Hebrew "kodesh" is allied to sanctify, which is translated by words such as dedicate, consecrate, hallow, and holy in the Scriptures. GOD wants us to know Him as Jehovah-M'Kaddesh, Jehovah who sets us apart unto Himself. In connection with man, Jehovah-M'Kaddesh (Jehovah who sanctifies), empowers us with His presence to set us apart for His service. The Lord wants us to be a holy nation (Exodus 19:5–6) that appreciates our high, holy, and heavenly calling (Exodus 31:13). We have no inherent holiness or righteousness apart from Him. God's command, "Sanctify yourselves" can be fulfilled only in the imparted and imputed righteousness of Christ, for, "I am the LORD which sanctify you."[35]

Are you holy as God is holy? Do you want to thrive in His divine grace?

When we determine to grow in sanctification and allow Yahweh M'Kaddesh to lead us to deeper places of divine grace, those around us will see the hope of Christ in us. Isn't that what we want? No matter where we find ourselves on the path of sanctification, it is encouraging to remember that God's not done with us yet. "God, who began the good work within you, will continue his work until it is finally finished on the day when Christ Jesus returns" (Philippians 1:6, NLT).

Let's Pray

Lord My Sanctifier, Yahweh M'Kaddesh, please help me to live a life worthy of You, a life that will please You in every way. Help me to bear fruit in every good work, to grow in the knowledge of You, and to be strengthened with all power according to Your glorious might so that I will be a woman of endurance and patience. With joyful thanks and in Jesus's name I pray, amen.

Now It's Your Turn

Time for Reflection

- We hope this week of devotions left you amazed by the grace of God! He is our Savior and our Deliverer, Ysuah. When did you come to know Jesus as your Savior? If you are doing this study in a group or with a friend, take time to share testimonies of how each of you came to Christ.
- Sharon told a story about visiting Alcatraz and meeting former prisoner Jim Quillen. What is the difference between a prisoner on parole and a prisoner set free? (As a reminder, read what Paul tells all believers in Galatians 5:1.) Which one describes your relationship with Jesus more accurately?
- God offers forgiveness to every heart that confesses sin and believes in His Son Jesus Christ for salvation. Read Ephesians 2:8: "For it is by grace you have been saved, through faith—and this not from yourselves, it is the gift of God." How would you explain the difference between *grace* and *faith* as they apply to your life?
- The noise of life can be so loud. We are right there with you in trying to hit the Mute button each day, yet failing on many occasions. When we stop to center our hearts on God and listen to stories of His grace, redemptive beauty drowns out the noise. He is such a wonderful Redeemer! Can you think of a way that God has woven redemption into your story?

- Job's life teaches us so many valuable lessons: that pain is no respecter of persons, that God cares for His people, and that knowing God is more important than knowing the *why* behind our wonders. Which of these three truths resonates most with you today?
- On Day 4 of this week, Sharon mentioned that *grace* is receiving a blessing you don't deserve, while *mercy* is *not* receiving the punishment that you *do* deserve. List three examples of both the mercy and the grace that you have received in your life.

Mercy	**Grace**
______________________	______________________
______________________	______________________
______________________	______________________

- We also looked at this passage: "In him we have redemption through his blood, the forgiveness of sins, in accordance with the riches of God's grace that he lavished on us with all wisdom and understanding" (Ephesians 1:7–8).

  Look up the word *lavish* in a dictionary. What picture does this give you of God's love for you?
- In Gwen's devotion about Yahweh M'Kaddesh, the Lord My Sanctifier, she unpacked some current cultural tendencies that allow electronics and other distractions to rob us of time and keep us from God. Let's get practical: confess any e-habits or distractions of yours that are sinful, indulgent, or inappropriate. What type of accountability could help you with this?
- Read, meditate on, and discuss The Message's paraphrase of David's prayer to the Lord found in Psalm 51:10–12: "God, make a fresh start in me, shape a Genesis week from the chaos

of my life. Don't throw me out with the trash, or fail to breathe holiness in me. Bring me back from gray exile, put a fresh wind in my sails!"

What would an answer to this prayer look like in your life?

Wrap up your response time with prayer. Move from confession, to adoration, to thanksgiving, and end with your petitions (personal prayer needs).

Going Deeper with God

List: the attributes and names of God with their meanings that were covered this week.

1. ______________________________
2. ______________________________
3. ______________________________
4. ______________________________
5. ______________________________

Read and **respond:** Write your own words of praise to the following verses.

> Who is a God like you,
> who pardons sin and forgives the transgression
> of the remnant of his inheritance?
> You do not stay angry forever
> but delight to show mercy. (Micah 7:18)

> But you are a forgiving God, gracious and compassionate,
> slow to anger and abounding in love. (Nehemiah 9:17)

Read: Ephesians 5:1–20.

Worship: Gwen co-wrote a song that invites God to invade our hearts with His holiness. It's called "Restore." Take a moment to listen to and pray through the song here: www.girlfriendsingod.com/2011/restore-us-o-god/.

Your GiG *Knowing God by Name* Journal

Spend a few moments contemplating and journaling about some of the scriptural truths that moved your heart as you read the devotions this week. Then use the space below to collect your thoughts or write a prayer of response to God.

absent 4-14

Dr. Mahmood 9:30
River

Guide me in your truth and teach me, for you are God my Savior, and my hope is in you all day long. (*Psalm 25:5*)

The Potter
Yatsar

Mary Southerland

Today's Truth

But Lord, you are our father. We are like clay, and you are the potter; your hands made us all. (Isaiah 64:8, NCV)

Friend to Friend

When our daughter was preschool age, one of her favorite activities was playing with clay. Danna often pulled her little stepstool over to the closet where the clay was stored and almost ceremoniously hauled out the boxes of brightly colored clay. It was like watching a commissioned artist prepare her canvas for the beauty it was about to receive. With great concentration and effort, Danna's little fingers pried open each box. She then thoughtfully and deliberately chose several lumps of clay and lined them up on the kitchen table where, with the seriousness of an experienced artist, she began to work.

For hours at a time, I would hear Danna singing while pounding, molding, stretching, and creating her unique clay world. Animals, people, flowers, and aliens emerged from the lumps of clay. When she was satisfied that her work was done, Danna announced it was time to "put them up." Translation: it was time to exhibit her clay masterpieces for her dad and brother to see when they came home. Danna met Dan and Jered at the door, took their hands, and escorted them to see her works of art. Then she waited for Dan and Jered to offer the mandatory "oohs" and "aahs" while applauding the artist who created them.

Danna's designs remained on display until they grew hard and brittle. Together, she and I then broke each creation apart, generously sprinkled every piece with water, and placed them back in their containers, allowing the clay to soften until she had another project in mind.

When it comes to spiritual matters, God is the Potter, the Creator, and we are the clay. Like Danna with her creations, He uses the circumstances of our lives to pound, mold, stretch, and shape us according to His vision alone.

God used the relationship between a potter and his clay to illustrate to the prophet Jeremiah His sovereignty and how He works in the lives of His children to accomplish His perfect plan:

> So I went down to the potter's house, and I saw him working at the wheel. But the pot he was shaping from the clay was marred in his hands; so the potter formed it into another pot, shaping it as seemed best to him.
>
> Then the word of the Lord came to me: "...Can I not do with you as this potter does?" declares the Lord. "Like clay in the hand of the potter, so are you in my hand, O house of Israel." (Jeremiah 18:3–6)

Just as in the days of Jeremiah, God still longs for His children to find and live out His mind-blowing plan for our lives—a plan that is far beyond anything we can possibly imagine or conceive on our own. And just as the children of Israel rebelled against God's plan, we tend to doubt His heart and think our frail human plans are better. We sometimes willingly submit to the gentle pressure of the Potter's hands, and other times we dig in our heels and refuse to budge.

Jeremiah understood that God was the Potter, *yatsar* in Hebrew, and had total control over the shape of the clay. "Can the pot say of the potter, 'He knows nothing'?" (Isaiah 29:16). Of course not, but we often forget that truth. How foolish it would be for the clay to grumble or rebel, but we do! Still, the Potter is faithful and so patient as He continues to mold the clay. If the clay begins to harden in its unfinished state, the Potter loves the clay enough to let it be crushed by the pressures of life. He then sprinkles it with the replenishing water of His presence and power and begins to mold His creation again. The Potter never tires of His work, and He never gives up on the potential that was lovingly tucked into our very being from the moment we were conceived in the heart and mind of God.

Because God is a loving Father who is more committed to our character than He is to our comfort, godly discipline must often come into play. Although God has the ability to directly give us understanding, His usual teaching method involves more of a hands-on approach. We gain wisdom as God teaches us His Word and then follows through with application in our daily lives.

The only way for us to become all God desires us to be is to remain pliable in the Potter's hands. When we try to shape ourselves, we fail miserably and often settle for so much less than God has in mind. The Potter wants to create something *eternally* beautiful. In fact, He wants to make us more like His Son, Jesus!

The story is told of a group of women who met each week to study the Bible, hoping to learn more about the nature and character of God and how He works in our lives. The women were puzzled and even a little troubled by the description of God they found in Malachi 3:3: "He will sit as a refiner and purifier of silver." One of the women offered to do a little research on the subject and report back to the group at their next meeting. The woman found a local silversmith and made an appointment to observe him at work, explaining that she was particularly interested in the process of refining silver. She watched as the craftsman carefully selected a piece of silver for his demonstration. She thought the piece of silver was already beautiful, but evidently the silversmith saw something she could not see. As he held the silver over the furnace, the craftsman explained that in refining silver, the silver had to be placed in the middle of the fire where the flames were hottest so all the impurities would be burned away.

The woman was silent as her thoughts drifted to the fiery trials she was facing in her own life. Honestly, she did not get it. Why would a loving God allow His children to suffer when He could so easily deliver them? In fact, why does God even allow bad things to happen to people who are seeking Him and trying to live for Him?

The woman asked the silversmith if it was true that he had to sit in front of the fire the whole time the silver was being refined. "Oh yes!" he replied. "I cannot take my eyes off the silver. If it is left in the furnace even a moment too long, it will be destroyed." The woman suddenly understood the beauty and comfort of Malachi 3:3: "He will sit as a refiner and purifier of silver."

If we could only trust that His shaping is so much better than anything we could ever create! But in our pride, we honestly think we can do better. The world says we should never give up our rights, because if we do, we will lose everything. God says if we surrender all to Him, we will gain everything that is eternally important.

All of us have rough edges that need to be removed. We may

even need to be broken and crushed so the Potter's masterful hands can begin again. I have been there many times and can honestly look back and say that the beauty God eventually brought forth was worth the pain.

Total surrender demands that we place ourselves in the Potter's hands with no agenda, no preset conditions—giving Him permission to bend us, break us, and change us. As we give up control to Him, like a Master Craftsman He begins to work patiently and lovingly, with a specific plan and one-of-a-kind design in mind. He works through circumstances as well as people, through joy and pain, victory and defeat. He filters every part of our situation through His plan, to create in us a life of worth and meaning and purpose.

When we try to direct our lives according to our own agendas and plans, we experience only discontent and frustration. Our souls long for more and our hearts cry out, "Is this all there is?" The truth is that nothing and no one but God can bring us the peace and joy for which we are searching. Are you ready to become the clay, surrendering your broken life to the Potter's loving hands? Today is the day!

Let's Pray

Lord, I am tired of trying to live life in my own power. I come to You as the Potter. I am the clay. Right now, I give up and surrender my life completely to You. I choose Your plan over mine. I give You permission to mold me and make me what You want me to be. I will wait before You and seek Your direction. In Jesus's name, amen.

Day 2

The Lord My Restorer
Yahweh El Ashiyb

Gwen Smith

Today's Truth

He leads me beside quiet waters, he restores my soul. (Psalm 23:2–3)

Friend to Friend

At times laundry takes over my house. Piles build up, though I try to stay on top of them. Many of the clothes are clean and even folded, but not put away. That tricky put-away part is always hard for me.

Then there are the socks. Oh, the socks! They burden me so. It causes me to wonder. Does an unseen sock nation exist? Are sock soldiers on a secret mission to destroy my testimony and drive me crazy? Divide and conquer. That's what they do! Why can't socks just behave? Why can't they ever stay in pairs, and where am I supposed to put the socks that remain unmatched? *Sigh.*

Unmatched socks and folded-but-not-put-away laundry sometimes linger for days in irritating little piles before I make time to deal with them. All the while their nagging presence leaves me tied up in knots.

I've come to realize that my days can be a lot like my laundry situation. At times they get piled up with *busy.* Sabbath gets squeezed out. Now, when I say *Sabbath,* I mean the priority of coming before the Lord just to sit with Him...quietly...expectantly...to listen...to be restored. Though I do include God in my days and breathe prayers throughout them, when I don't *sit* before the Lord and exercise the spiritual discipline of *being quiet* before God, my heart becomes a big frazzled knot.

It had been one of those weeks. Knots. Knots. Knots. Then I finally remembered the power of quiet. I remembered my Restorer. As I sat in the cool still of the morning with a hot mug of coffee in my hand and the warming presence of God in my soul, the busy in my heart began to drift away. Direction came. Joy resounded. Mercy rained. Peace, deep peace, fell.

The Spirit of God transformed my soul, my thoughts, my goals, and my day. *This is where it goes. This is where my busy belongs.* Like the unending piles of laundry, every line of my to-do list needed to be put away in its proper place—in God's hands. Then—order, *soul* order...peace, *compelling* peace...joy, *divine* joy...and restoration—it all came.

I sat in wonder.

Still.

In His presence.

Convicted of my failure to remember the power of being quiet before the Lord. *Of course. This is where my soul belongs. I knew that. Lord, forgive me. Oh, how I'm thankful for Your daily mercy showers.* I was met in my mess by Yahweh El Ashiyb, the Lord My Restorer. And He restored order out of the chaos of my life.

David spoke of God as his Restorer in the Bible. Now *there's* a guy I can relate to! He came from a big family. Me too. He dreamed big dreams and thought big thoughts about God. Me too. He was a music dude who lived to chase melody and verse, loved passionately, and asked endless questions of God. Me too. At one point, his ego became too big for his britches, and he messed up royally. Me too. He mopped the floor of his misery with confession, fully acknowledging his failures, fully humbled by God's scandalous grace. Me too.

On the other side of his life's knots, unmatched socks, and messy failures, David knew God as both his Redeemer and Restorer. Redemption precedes restoration for each of us, just as obedience precedes blessing. In Psalm 23, David celebrated the God who brought him restoration beside the quiet waters of His presence: "The Lord is my shepherd, I shall not be in want. He makes me lie down in green pastures, he leads me beside quiet waters, he restores my soul" (verses 1–3).

David found soul-deep restoration when he spent time with God. In fact, we cannot experience complete restoration apart from Him. Notice that David did not relate soul restoration to a change in circumstances but to a shift in his heart position. He experienced powerful renewal in the presence of the Prince of Peace.

When David parked beside still waters and got with God, Yahweh El Ashiyb, he gained guidance for his day, courage for his challenges, and comfort for his burdens. "He guides me in paths of righteousness for his name's sake. Even though I walk through the valley of the shadow of death, I will fear no evil, for you are with me; your rod and your staff, they comfort me" (verses 3–4).

Each of us is invited to experience God as our Restorer. To know the renewal we long for each day. Jesus invited us personally when He said, "Come to me, all you who are weary and burdened, and I will give you rest. Take my yoke upon you and learn from me, for I am gentle and humble in heart, and you will find rest for your souls. For my yoke is easy and my burden is light" (Matthew 11:28–30).

When our lives get too chaotic—when the laundry piles up in our homes and our dizzy days pile up in our hearts—we often forget the restorative power of quiet. The power of being still before God. The power of listening, expecting, pouring out our souls—and receiving rest from Yahweh El Ashiyb. In His presence our busy gets put away and we are restored.

How great is our God?

Take some time to power down and be still before Him right now. Remember the power of quiet as you accept the renewal invitation of Jesus and exchange your knots for His peace and restoration.

Let's Pray

Dear Lord, El Ashiyb, Restorer of my soul, Your mercy is fresh each day, and Your grace piles higher than all my laundry and all of my heart-woes. Thank You, Lord! I'm here. Please align my heart to Yours. Quiet me with Your love, direction, peace, and restoration today. In Jesus's name, amen.

The Lord Will Provide

Yahweh Yireh

Mary Southerland

Today's Truth

Abraham named the place Yahweh-Yireh (which means "the Lord will provide"). To this day, people still use that name as a proverb: "On the mountain of the Lord it will be provided." (Genesis 22:14, NLT)

Friend to Friend

As I worked through the seemingly endless number of e-mails, my heart grew heavy and my soul cried out to God. So many women in so much pain. I could feel their fear and confusion in every word they wrote. Though their circumstances were all different, each was really asking the same question, "Where are You, God?"

I was already tired and overwhelmed, having just returned from speaking at a conference in an area of the country where the economy had taken a nosedive. So many of the prayer requests were centered around one deep need: the provision of God. And honestly, I was struggling with the same question in my own life.

I hurt. The doctors said it was fibromyalgia and that the medical world doesn't really understand the disease, so my treatment options were "iffy" at best. I had a lot of questions, but no one seemed to have any answers.

I was afraid. Due to a family emergency, we didn't have enough money to pay the rent and had just learned that both of my husband's parents had cancer. A boatload of unknowns stretched before us.

I was lonely. I have great friends and a support group most women would envy, but at that moment, I felt as if no one really understood what I was going through.

I too cried out, "Where are You, God?"

He gently whispered, *I am right here, daughter. I am Your Yahweh Yireh. Remember Abraham?* I did remember, but I obviously needed a refresher course in faith. I grabbed my Bible and turned to Genesis 22 to read the faith story I have read so many times in my life. But this time, I saw Abraham through different eyes.

When God asked him to sacrifice his son of promise, Isaac, Abraham must have hurt in a way I will never understand. His soul must have wanted to scream the question, "Why, God?" But in total obedience, Abraham walked through his fear and doubt and pain, and prepared to do the unthinkable—because God had asked him to. He, his servants, and his son Isaac began the journey to Mount Moriah where the sacrifice was to be made.

I can only imagine the turmoil in Abraham's heart when Isaac asked where the sacrificial lamb was. With a heart of resolve and pure faith, Abraham promised his son that God would provide. When they reached the place where the servants were to wait, Abraham told the servants, "Stay here with the donkey.... The boy and I will travel a little farther. We will worship there, and then we will come right back" (Genesis 22:5, NLT). The truth hit me right between my faith and my fear. Abraham said "we" will be back. I don't believe Abraham was in denial. Nor do I believe God had already told him what the ultimate plan was. Abraham was simply counting on Yahweh Yireh to make a way that would honor God—no matter what the cost might be to Abraham.

Abraham and Isaac proceeded to the appointed place where Abraham gently laid his son on the altar. I can only imagine the confusion in Isaac's eyes as he gazed up at his father holding a knife. Isaac was a teenage boy, not a child. He could have easily resisted his father. He could have said that he was not about to die just to prove a point. No way! But Isaac had faith too. He trusted his daddy, even when he had no clue what was about to happen. Isaac was sure of his father's love and care. And that was enough for both Abraham and Isaac. It was also enough for God.

Just as Abraham drew back the knife to end the life of his son, the angel of the Lord stopped him. Isaac would live! Why? Abraham had proven faithful and obedient, even when he didn't understand God's plan—even when he could not logically explain the seemingly appalling command of a loving God.

Abraham spotted a ram caught in the thicket and offered the ram as a sacrifice in place of Isaac. Abraham then worshiped God, praising Him for His perfect provision. "Abraham named the place Yahweh-Yireh (which means 'the LORD will provide'). To this day, people still use that name as a proverb: 'On the mountain of the LORD it will be provided" (verse 14, NLT). Abraham's obedience led to God's provision—the provision of Yahweh Yireh.

Wow! Talk about a faith story. Yahweh Yireh indeed!

As I contemplated Abraham's amazing faith, God gently nudged my heart, reminding me that I too needed to lay my "Isaac" on the altar of faith and trust Yahweh Yireh. "But, Lord," I argued, "Abraham is *the man* when it comes to faith. I don't have that kind of faith. What do I do?"

God is so sweet and so kind and so very patient. His Spirit nudged my heart once again. *Mary, think about the Israelites.* Now we're talking! I can *so* relate to the Israelites. I turned to Joshua 3 and found myself in very familiar company.

The Israelites were camped on the bank of the Jordan River. Forty years earlier, they had escaped from Egypt, and they'd been wandering around in the wilderness ever since. All their needs had been met by God. They had witnessed miracle after miracle, and now they could see Canaan, the Promised Land. However, there was a problem.

A huge river stood between the Israelites and the Promised Land. There was no way around it. To make things worse, it was flood season, and the usual places to cross were submerged under deep, rushing water. The Israelites knew God could stop the river right before their eyes or could throw a bridge across it. But He didn't. Instead, He told Joshua that the priests were to pick up the ark of the covenant and stand in the river. What? Sounds crazy, I know, but God was not kidding!

God promised to make a dry path through the river, but the priests had never seen such a thing happen. In fact, they hadn't even been born when the Red Sea was parted, and there were no reruns of *The Ten Commandments* at the local Wilderness Theater. God was asking them to carry the ark of the covenant and cross that river! I can only imagine their fear and questions. God was asking them to step out in faith as never before.

I wonder if the Israelites had a great deal of faith in God at that moment. Probably not, but they had just enough faith to take that first step. And that was enough.

> During harvest the Jordan overflows its banks. When the priests carrying the Ark came to the edge of the river and stepped into the water, the water upstream stopped flowing. It stood up in a heap.... So the people crossed the river. (Joshua 3:15–16, NCV)

Notice: God did *nothing* until those toes touched the water. That first step was all God needed to see. Many times, we won't take the first step because we're afraid we won't be able to make the whole journey. But the paths our lives will travel aren't determined by what we are able to do; they're all about whether or not we have faith in our Provider.

Don't wait until you *believe* it all.

Don't wait until you can *see* it all.

Don't wait until you *understand* it all.

Step out in childlike faith and put your trust in God.

He is Yahweh Yireh.

He will provide.

Let's Pray

Father, I come to You today, wanting to know You and follow You. I'm afraid and my faith is small, but I'm placing the faith I do have in You, Lord. I trust You to strengthen and grow that faith and help me become a fully devoted follower who pleases and honors You. In Jesus's name, amen.

Day 4

Husband
Ish

Sharon Jaynes

Today's Truth

For your Maker is your husband—the LORD Almighty is his name—the Holy One of Israel is your Redeemer; he is called the God of all the earth. (Isaiah 54:5)

Friend to Friend

I was five years old, just a wisp of a girl living in a dream world all my own. On one particular afternoon, I gathered my supplies and prepared for the big day. First, I wrapped a long white sheet around my slender body and tossed the excess over my shoulder and down my back. Then I draped a bath-sized towel over the crown of my head like a veil and clutched a bouquet of plastic flowers to my chest. I stood at the end of my home's long hallway, and the processional began. I could almost hear the organ playing "Here Comes the Bride," as I sashayed down the "aisle" with imaginary friends and family looking on.

Little girls and big girls dream about the day they will become brides. And for many, that dream doesn't turn out the way they had hoped. But here is some good news—some great news, actually: no matter what your marital status this side of heaven—never married, once married, happily married, widowed, or divorced—God is your holy Husband who longs to protect you, provide for you, and cherish you through all the ups and downs of life.

We first see God's name as Ish, or Husband, in the book of Isaiah: "For your Maker is your husband—the LORD Almighty is his name—the Holy One of Israel is your Redeemer; he is called the God of all the earth" (54:5). We see it again in the book of Hosea as God speaks about drawing the unfaithful Israel back into His arms: "'In that day,' declares the LORD, 'you will call me "my husband";... I will betroth you to me forever; I will betroth you in righteousness and justice, in love and compassion. I will betroth you in faithfulness, and you will acknowledge the LORD'" (2:16, 19–20).

In the New Testament, Jesus is also referred to as the husband for His bride, the Church. The Greek word is *aner,* and it is translated "husband" or "bridegroom."[36] When Jesus was questioned about why His disciples did not fast, He replied, "How can the guests of the bridegroom mourn while he is with them? The time will come when the bridegroom will be taken from them; then they will fast" (Matthew 9:15). And in the book of Revelation, Jesus's return is referred to as the "wedding of the Lamb" (Revelation 19:6–9).

I asked my husband what visual image forms in his mind when he reads that he is part of the bride of Christ.

"Nothing, really," he replied.

Granted, I can't picture Steve walking down the aisle in a pearl-studded wedding gown. But oh, sister, I can see myself waltzing down the aisle to meet my Jesus. Can't you? What a blessing God has given His female image-bearers as the bride of Christ, our Husband![37]

In ancient Jewish tradition, the father chose a bride for his son. If the girl's father accepted the proposal of marriage, the groom paid to her family a "bride price" of a few cows, a couple of sheep, or perhaps some gold trinkets. The couple drank from a cup of wine to seal the marriage covenant between them, and would not drink of it again until the day of the wedding ceremony. Then the groom left his betrothed and went back to his father's house to build a home for her. Once the home was completed to the satisfaction of the groom's father, the young man returned to whisk away his bride. Usually this took place in the middle of the night, with torch-toting groomsmen whooping and hollering to let her know they were on their way. The bride's responsibility was to be prepared, to be ready at all times.

And so it is with you and your Groom. God has chosen you to be the bride for His Son (Ephesians 1:4). Jesus paid the ultimate bride price when He gave His very life on the cross (1 Corinthians 6:20). At the Last Supper, after Jesus and His disciples had broken the bread and drunk the wine, He explained to them, "I will not drink of this fruit of the vine from now on until that day when I drink it anew with you in my Father's kingdom" (Matthew 26:29).

And where is Jesus right now? He is preparing your home. "In my Father's house are many rooms," Jesus said. "If it were not so, I would have told you. I am going there to prepare a place for you. And if I go and prepare a place for you, I will come back and take you to be with me that you also may be where I am" (John 14:2–3). And when His Father says it is time, Jesus will come back like a "thief in the night" to whisk away his bride (1 Thessalonians 5:2).

Doesn't that just give you chills!

Let me tell you about one particular "wedding day" that captured my heart. The sun shone brightly as the daffodils danced in the gentle breeze, nodding their happy faces in conversation. A choir of robins, cardinals, and finches sang rounds of cheerful melodies, which floated through a clear blue sky that perfectly matched the bride's sparkling eyes. The air had that unusual crisp quality of spring, reminding us of the chill from winter's past and the warmth of summer's promise.

It was Easter Sunday, the day the Groom had chosen to be joined to His beloved. As in the Jewish custom of old, He had proposed to His young maiden and then promptly gone away to prepare a home for her. On this day His Father had signaled that the home was ready and He could go to get His bride.

Iris had been waiting for her Husband to come and take her to the wonderful home that He had prepared for her. *How like Him to pick Easter,* she thought to herself. *My favorite day of the year.* She smiled as she heard Him coming, and her heart fluttered with the anticipation of seeing His face.

She wore a white dress with flecks of blue and carried a bouquet of pink carnations and white mums with a spray of asparagus fern as wispy as her baby-fine hair. A sweet smile spread across her face as she saw her beloved Jesus hold out His strong hand to help her cross the threshold of the temporal and into the hall of eternity. She walked into His loving embrace and drank in the loveliness of her surroundings, which He had perfectly described in His many letters.

On Easter Sunday 1997, my husband's dear, sweet, seventy-four-year-old aunt Iris went home to be with the Lord. As we all gathered around to say our last good-byes, I could not manage to be mournful. Yes, I was going to miss her, but Iris had never been married on this side of eternity. I envisioned her joining the Lord as the bride of Christ. For me, it was not a funeral but a wedding. It was what she had always longed for...a dream come true.

In Isaiah 61:3, the prophet describes what God will do for the bride. He will bestow on her a crown of beauty instead of ashes, anoint her with the oil of gladness instead of mourning, and place on her shoulders a garment of praise instead of a spirit of despair. Whether or not you ever marry this side of heaven, God will one day place the crown of a royal bride on your head. So lift your head, dear one, and accept your crown from the King of kings. His name is Ish—Husband—and He longs to take you in His arms, not simply "for as long as you both shall live," but for all eternity.

Let's Pray

Yahweh Ish, thank You for caring for me as a husband cares for his bride. Thank You for Your protection, provision, and never-ending love. I rest in the knowledge that You are my sacred Ish, not simply "till death do us part," but for all eternity. In Jesus's name, amen.

Day 5

The Builder and Architect

Mary Southerland

Today's Truth

For he [Abraham] was looking forward to the city with foundations, whose architect and builder is God. (Hebrews 11:10)

Friend to Friend

Our son was born to be a builder. From the time he could hold a red plastic hammer in his toddler-sized hands, Jered began hammering imaginary nails into the coffee table and "fixing" anything in our house that he thought was broken. No wooden surface was safe from Jered's scrutiny or design. Since my husband enjoyed woodworking, he decided to build Jered a miniature workbench beside his own. Several nights each week, Dan and Jered headed to the garage to pound and hammer and do what they called "man stuff." I thought it was cute—a philosophy that would drastically change in the years to come.

I knew we had a true builder on our hands when Jered built a clubhouse *inside* our garage. And what a clubhouse it was. For weeks, Jered scrounged wood and what he called "treasures" from neighborhood Dumpsters and construction sites. The house was made largely of plywood but boasted a carpeted floor, four walls, and a roof. Jered cut out windows and found a rusty old-but-still-slightly-working window air-conditioning unit to keep him and his friends cool during their club meetings. The structure was truly a work of art!

Jered built a jewelry box for my birthday and a toy box that held his prized Mutant Ninja Turtles. If we needed storage cabinets in our garage, Jered built them. He designed and built a queen-sized bunk bed over a built-in desk and bookshelves to conserve space in his room. We no longer bought furniture. Jered simply built it. Looking back, I didn't realize those plastic tools would pave the way for our son's career. Today, he owns a construction business and is a master carpenter and builder.

Jered reminds me of another young man who was destined to become a builder: Jesus. His earthly father, Joseph, likely taught Jesus everything he'd learned in his work as a master carpenter. In those days, it was not uncommon for the son to carry on his father's business. I often wonder if Jesus didn't have a little workbench beside Joseph's. I imagine Jesus probably followed His daddy around, hammering alongside His father's true blows. Joseph may have had to remove a few stray nails driven by Jesus and even repair a few of his Son's "jobs." Did Jesus make a jewelry box for His mother, or did He build a piece of furniture that Mary treasured like I treasure everything Jered has ever built for our home? Of course, no matter how much or little He may have labored alongside Joseph, Jesus shared wholly in the work and nature of His Father—God, the ultimate architect and builder, the Master Creator.

When the word *creator* is used in the Bible, it always refers to Elohim the Creator, "The Lord…, the Creator of the ends of the earth" (Isaiah 40:28). God often works like an architect in our lives as He implements His plans through our daily circumstances and builds us up through others. The Bible is filled with God's handiwork as a builder and architect:

- Genesis 1 is an amazing account of God at work as the architect of our planet.
- Noah's ark was more than just a way to escape the disastrous flood. It was a masterpiece in workmanship given to Noah by God.
- The tabernacle was a beautiful place of worship but also displayed symbols detailing much of God's plan for the children of Israel.
- Solomon's temple describes the permanent home for God built by David's son based on the design provided by God Himself.
- Revelation offers a detailed blueprint of heaven—the work of God's own hands—right down to the kinds of stones embedded in the heavenly walls.

All these examples and more confirm that God is the Master Creator. But His greatest creations are not of wood or stone. God was and is the Creator of eternal masterpieces like you and me. His design for our lives is second to none, is detailed in the Word of God, and is without flaw as God uses it to mold us into His image. The Church is built upon the foundation Jesus laid down with His earthly life, death, burial, and resurrection. In Hebrews 3:4 we read, "For every house is built by someone, but God is the builder of everything." The Greek word translated as *builder* is *kataskeuazo,* a verb meaning "to prepare, establish, make ready, construct."[38] Scholars agree that the house referred to in this verse is not a literal house but a spiritual house.

Yes, God is the Master architect and builder of eternity. We are the Church and God is the builder of our lives and the architect of our souls. We are His living masterpieces.

God's work often includes a phase of remodeling when parts of our lives need refinishing or repair. I don't like this process of remodeling, in houses or in life.

I once promised myself I would never buy a fixer-upper house. I want everything to be fixed *before* I move in. But there we were, buying a house that needed so much work even the Realtor couldn't believe we were serious. Why didn't someone stop me? No one did, so the sale was made and we went to work. Actually, my son and husband went to work while I went slightly crazy. I had no idea how horrible the process of remodeling could be. Layers of dirt and ugliness were stripped away. Rotten kitchen cabinets were torn from the walls, and rusty appliances were replaced. We basically gutted the whole place and rebuilt it—while living in it. I was not happy!

I will never forget the day I woke to see a toilet sitting at the foot of our bed. I firmly resolved to never set foot in another house that required so much work. I am so thankful God doesn't feel that way about me.

There have been times when I wondered why God didn't just demolish the old me and build a new one. Then He did just that, through a two-year battle with clinical depression. While sitting at the bottom of that dark and slimy pit, the Father lovingly stripped away old fears and insecurities. From the walls of my heart, He tore the rotten attitudes, undisciplined thoughts, and unholy desires that had walked me to the edge of my pit and pushed me in. He replaced rusty old dreams with His perfect plans and basically gutted my life to build a new one, a better one, and a stronger, more purpose-filled one.

Yes, our Creator knows us best and loves us most. There are no accidents with God. Before we were ever conceived in the heart and mind of man, we were conceived in the heart and mind of God.

Wanted, loved, and planned since before the world began. He lovingly, purposefully created us in response to that plan.

"'For I know the plans I have for you,' says the Lord. 'They are plans for good and not for disaster, to give you a future and a hope'" (Jeremiah 29:11, NLT).

I know that each of us endures seasons when the plan of God seems completely wrong and we simply don't understand. Every moment is pregnant with uncertainty, and our hearts are paralyzed by fear and doubt. We are treading water in the stormy seas of life, desperately longing to see God walking toward us on the treacherous waves, rescue in His hand. It is in those shadowed moments that we must choose to trust the Plan Maker, the Master Designer, even though our faith is small and we cannot understand the plan or make sense of His divine blueprints. His ways are higher than our ways. His thoughts are higher than our thoughts. And someday, every one of our question marks will be yanked into exclamation points when we see that plan as God sees it—"perfect and complete, lacking in nothing" (James 1:4, ESV).

Today, girlfriend, set aside your meager agenda. Lay down your limited life arrangement and look for God, your architect and builder, to meet you at the point of surrender with the perfect tools to execute His perfect plan.

Let's Pray

Father, please forgive me when I stubbornly choose to ignore Your plan. Thank You for always being ready to rescue me from my own selfish desires and decisions. Help me remember that Your plan is the highest and best plan for my life, and give me the strength to follow You. I want to honor and please You, Lord. In Jesus's name, amen.

Now It's Your Turn

Time for Reflection

- This week we read about the prophet Jeremiah's visit to the potter's house. God is the Potter and we are the clay. He has a beautiful plan for each life and can be trusted. Are you living according to God's plan for your life or according to your own plan? Which of the following best describes your current level of submission to the Potter's hands and plans?

  A. My way or the highway, baby! (Honestly, God's plan is not even on my radar.)

  B. I like God's plan, but I like my plan a good bit better. (True confessions…control issues!)

  C. I try to let the Potter's plan prevail but sometimes forget that I'm the clay. (He needs my opinion, right? Right?)

  D. I surrender all! (Spin the wheel, Lord! Carve away! Mold me! Shape me! Move me! Do Your thang!)

- God is Yahweh El Ashiyb, our Restorer. When chaos, calamity, or busyness tangle your heart in knots, the Lord is available to bring you peace. Soul-deep restoration is found when we get with God. When was the last time you were still—really still—before God?

- On a scale of 1 to 5, how satisfied are you with your current restoration level? (1 = unsatisfied, 5 = completely satisfied) ____

  Do you believe there is a direct correlation between the level of your peace and the consistency of your God-dwelling? Why or why not?

- What benefits do you experience when you prioritize spending personal time with the Lord?

- Look up Zephaniah 3:17 and fill in the blanks below.

  "The Lord your God is ________ ________, he is mighty to save. He will take ________ ________ in you, he will ________ you with his ________, he will ________ over you with ________."

  What does this verse tell you about God?

- Another name of God featured in a devotion this week was Yahweh Yireh, our Provider. What is the greatest problem or need in your life today? Do you believe that God is able to meet that need?

- What steps do you need to take to face that problem or need with faith instead of fear? Are there any barriers keeping you from trusting God and stepping out in faith? If so, what needs to be done to remove those barriers?

- Read Psalm 127:1: "Unless the Lord builds a house, the work of the builders is wasted" (NLT). Compare the truths of this verse to your life, thinking of your life as the house. Describe three foundational components of your life-house.

  1. ________________________________
  2. ________________________________
  3. ________________________________

- Look up 1 Corinthians 3:16 and fill in the blanks below.

"Don't you know that you yourselves are ______________ ______________ and that ______________ lives in you?"

How does this verse impact the way you live, think, and act? Should it impact your life? Pause to reflect on this. If you are in a group, discuss it.

- Wrap up your response time with prayer. Move from confession, to adoration, to thanksgiving, and end with your petitions (personal prayer needs).

Going Deeper with God

List: the attributes and names of God with their meanings that were covered this week.

1. ______________
2. ______________
3. ______________
4. ______________
5. ______________

Read and **reflect:** Psalm 139.

- What does this passage of Scripture say to you about God's plan for your life?
- Do you think certain areas of your life reflect the image of God? Which areas? In what way(s)?
- Now get brutally honest. Which areas of your life do not reflect the image of God?
- Are you willing to surrender those areas to Him so He can "remodel" them?

YOUR GIG *KNOWING GOD BY NAME* JOURNAL

Spend a few moments contemplating and journaling about some of the scriptural truths that moved your heart as you read the devotions this week. Then use the space below to collect your thoughts or write a prayer of response to God.

4-21-16

Janet - knee surgery Monday
in our group

Helen & John Rambo

Dawnette Nardini

Katy Carter - miscarriage
D&C

Safe travels

Robin Threadgill

Baby Calvin

Fran Barger - Brenda's
94 mother-in-law

(Hobbs)

But LORD, you are our father. We are like clay,
and you are the potter; your hands made us all.
(Isaiah 64:8, NCV*)*

Father
Abba

Sharon Jaynes

Today's Truth

I will be a Father to you, and you will be my sons and daughters, says the Lord Almighty. (2 Corinthians 6:18)

Friend to Friend

Once upon a time, not so very long ago or far away, a baby girl was born to parents who could not keep her. Neither parent was willing to release her for adoption, but neither was able to care for her. So while the legal system shuffled her case back and forth, the baby girl grew into a toddler in a foster home.

Her care was certainly adequate, her physical needs were met, and she never went hungry. Her clothes, though not new, were never dirty. Her toys, though not her own, were always sufficient. This little girl was not mistreated or abused, and yet, in her heart was a hollow space. She desperately wanted what she had never had: a mommy and a daddy of her own.

A few doors away from the foster home lived a kind couple with a teenage son. The family wanted a little girl, the little girl needed a family, and the details of a trying and lengthy adoption process were worked out. And while this little girl received a wonderful mommy and an adoring big brother, her relationship with her daddy was extra special.

Ashley was two years old when she entered his life. She was thin, pale, and clingy. By the time the adoption was finally complete, she was almost three. Ashley had never seen the ocean, eaten a Happy Meal, or slept in a bed in a room of her own.

When her new daddy took her to McDonald's for the first time, Ashley didn't play with the other children on the playground equipment. She was too busy asking them important questions: "Do you have a daddy? I have a daddy! See, that's my daddy over there," she exclaimed with excitement and wonder. "Isn't he wonderful?"

She approached another child. "What's your name?" she asked. "My name is Ashley Jordan *Ambrose,* just like my daddy. I'm named after my daddy!"

A few months after the adoption, Ashley traveled to the beach for her first family reunion. She was overwhelmed with excitement and pride. She had received so much so fast, and it was hard to take it all in. Ashley asked everyone she met if they were part of her family. "Are you my aunt?" "Are you my uncle?" "Are you my cousin?" She ran from person to person, showering hugs and kisses on her newly acquired family. "I love you!" she told them. "I love you all!"

Five years later, tanned, transformed, and confident, Ashley returned to the annual family reunion. This time she brought a scrapbook of pictures to share with anyone who would sit still long enough to look and listen.

"This is my story," she would say. "See, this is where I lived before Mommy and Daddy adopted me. They picked me out special.

See, this is my room now. It's all my own. And these are my toys and my own clothes, and here's a picture of my kitty and one of my dog and..."

Ashley has love overflowing for everyone, but no one ranks higher on her list than her daddy. He knows how to polish toenails, build sand castles, tie hair ribbons, hold her in the night—and he calls her his little princess.[39]

I love that story because, you see, I too have been adopted by my *heavenly* Father—and He calls *me* His little princess. And, friend, that is also true for you.

When I was a little girl, my father spent most of his waking hours working at his building-supply company, observing construction sites, and socializing with his colleagues and associates. Even though his place of business was only a few blocks from our home, his heart was miles away in a place I could not find.

My father didn't drink alcohol every day, but when he did, it consumed him. Rage always seemed to be hiding just beneath the surface of his tough skin, and when he drank, that rage spewed out like hot lava onto those around him. Unfortunately, my mother was the most common target. Many nights I crawled into bed, pulled the covers tightly under my chin or even over my head, and prayed that I would quickly fall asleep to shut out the noise of my parents yelling, fighting, and hitting.

I was afraid of my father. Even when he was sober, I kept my distance. At the same time, I observed how other daddies cherished their little girls. I saw them cuddle their daughters in their laps, hold their hands while walking in the park, or kiss their cheeks as they dropped them off at school in the mornings. And while I wasn't *fatherless,* I felt as though I were. Deep in my heart, I had a dream. I dreamed that one day I would have a daddy who loved me—not because I was pretty or made good grades or could play the piano well, but just because I was his.

Then one day, the dream came true. I discovered that I did have a Father who loved me—and so do you. God is your heavenly Father who loves you unconditionally, provides for you unreservedly, and protects you unceasingly.

In the New Testament, Jesus called God by the name Father more than any other name. And the Savior invites His followers to do the same.

When the disciples asked Jesus to teach them how to pray, He said:

> But when you pray, go into your room, close the door and pray to your *Father,* who is unseen. Then your *Father,* who sees what is done in secret, will reward you. And when you pray, do not keep on babbling like pagans, for they think they will be heard because of their many words. Do not be like them, for your *Father* knows what you need before you ask him.
>
> This, then, is how you should pray:
> "Our *Father* in heaven,
> hallowed be your name." (Matthew 6:6–9)

In reality, Jesus's invitation goes even deeper than the word *Father.* The word *Abba* is a term of endearment in a family circle and more akin to our word *dad* or *daddy.*[40]

Here's how Paul explained it in Galatians 4:6: "Because you are sons, God sent the Spirit of his Son into our hearts, the Spirit who calls out, '*Abba,* Father.'" Think about that for a moment. The God of the universe who created the heavens and the earth; who always has been and always will be; who is all knowing, all powerful, and present everywhere at once—that same God invites you to call Him Abba, Father!

J. I. Packer wrote, "For everything that Christ taught, everything that makes the New Testament new and better than the Old, everything that is distinctly Christian as opposed to merely Jewish, is summed up in the knowledge of the fatherhood of God."[41] The great I AM invites us to crawl up in His lap, become His child, and call Him Abba, Daddy. He said, "I will be a Father to you, and you will be my sons and daughters" (2 Corinthians 6:18).

My friend Gayle has a granddaughter named Carlie. Carlie and her best friend were born on the same day, and their moms were in hospital rooms right beside each other. Not only that, the two girls lived in the same apartment complex. However, unlike Carlie, her friend never knew her father. Her mom had boyfriends that came and went through the years, but she'd never known a real dad.

When Gayle kept Carlie on the weekends, sometimes her best friend came along. One day when both girls were about five years old, Gayle had both girls in the backseat when she was running an errand. Out of the blue, Carlie's little friend said, "I wish I had a daddy like you have a daddy."

And Carlie said, "Oh, you do have a Daddy."

"No, I don't. I want a daddy like you have a daddy. I wish I had a daddy."

"But you do have a Daddy," Carlie insisted. "We all have a Daddy. God is our Daddy. He's everybody's Daddy."

Gayle looked in her rearview mirror and saw Carlie's friend hold up her hands in exasperation. "Why has nobody ever told me this!"

How precious! I have a Daddy. You have a Daddy. God is your

Father, and He loves you more than you could ever know. You, my friend, are the apple of your Daddy's eye (Psalm 17:8).

Let's Pray

Heavenly Father, oh, how I love You. Thank You for adopting me into Your family and making me Your child. Thank You for being my heavenly Parent who loves me unconditionally, cares for me unendingly, and provides for all my needs. I am so blessed to be Your child. In Jesus's name, amen.

God of All Comfort

Paraklesis

Mary Southerland

Today's Truth

Blessed be the God and Father of our Lord Jesus Christ, the Father of mercies and God of all comfort, who comforts us in all our affliction so that we will be able to comfort those who are in any affliction with the comfort with which we ourselves are comforted by God. (2 Corinthians 1:3–4, NASB)

Friend to Friend

Allan Emery, who served for many years with the Billy Graham Evangelistic Association, shared an experience that made a deep impression on him as a young man. His father received a call saying a well-known Christian had been found drunk on the sidewalk in front of a local bar. Emery's father immediately sent his chauffeured limousine to pick up the man while his mother prepared the best guest room. Emery watched, wide-eyed, as the beautiful coverlets were turned down on the exquisite old four-poster bed, revealing monogrammed sheets.

"But, Mother," Emery protested, "he's drunk. He might even get sick."

"I know," his mother replied kindly, "but this man has slipped and fallen. When he comes to, he will be so ashamed. He will need all the compassion and loving encouragement we can give him."[42]

We all stumble and fall and, at one time or another, need someone who is willing to show us the love of God. The apostle Paul had certainly experienced God's compassion and wrote a letter to the church at Corinth, encouraging them to share that same compassion with those in need. One of the key words in this letter is *comfort* or *encouragement.* In the Greek, it means "called to one's side to help" and is used twenty-nine times in this letter alone.[43]

When trouble comes, we tend to look in all the wrong places for comfort, when what we should do is run straight into the arms of the source of all comfort: God. Isaiah 49:13 promises, "Shout for joy, O heavens; rejoice, O earth; burst into song, O mountains! For the Lord comforts his people and will have compassion on his afflicted ones." Where the world sees only a hopeless end, the Christian rejoices in an endless hope. We know that when a child of God is in the furnace, the Father keeps His hand on the thermostat and His eyes on His child. He monitors the heat, and He offers the comfort that is needed, just as He did in the life of Elijah.

You may recall Elijah's showdown with Ahab, which we discussed in Week 3, Day 3. Well, not long after he left that scene as the conquering hero, we find him under a juniper tree, wallowing in self-pity and begging God to let him die. Elijah had called down fire from heaven, proving the existence of the only true God, destroying idols and idol worshipers. Big stuff! In fact, it is my personal opinion that he should have been celebrating. So why was he discouraged? It was a woman, Jezebel, who was largely responsible for his discouragement.

Jezebel was the evil and influential wife of Ahab, king of Israel, and widely known as the real power behind her husband's throne.

Jezebel didn't worship the one true God of Israel. Instead, she was fanatical in her worship of the pagan god Baal and tried to impose her beliefs on the people of Israel. One man stood in her way: Elijah. As we saw, when he challenged the prophets of Baal to a showdown on Mount Carmel, God answered Elijah's prayer with a stream of fire from heaven. You would think a miracle like that would have convinced Ahab and Jezebel to believe in God. It didn't. In fact, Jezebel became furious. When she learned what had happened, she put a contract out on Elijah and swore he'd be dead within twenty-four hours. So the prophet went on the run, afraid for his life. Now stop and think about that for a moment.

Elijah had been in the presence of God. God had heard and answered Elijah's prayer, putting on an impressive fiery display for all to see. Idols had fallen. The prophets of Baal had either fled or been destroyed. And Elijah was worried about one angry woman? Clearly, he was tired and desperately needed the comfort of God. He found that comfort while sitting under a juniper tree, waiting in silence for God to show up. I know. God had already shown up in big ways for Elijah, but this time the despairing prophet needed a personal, one-on-one encounter with his Father. I've been there; haven't you?

When I went through my first major battle with clinical depression, I was amazed at the compassionate people God sent to encourage and comfort me. One of the most precious groups of encouragers was the elders of our church where my husband served as pastor. Dan and I shared what I was going through and asked the elders to pray, which they did. They then put feet to those prayers and came up with what they called the "Rescue Mary Plan."

Our church had five services each weekend, and because I was so emotionally frail, I never knew which service I would attend, or even if I could attend, until I was dressed and headed out the door.

Then I would call Dan to let him know I was on the way, and Dan relayed the message to the elders, who went into action. One would meet me at the car and escort me inside. Another would keep an eye on me during the service in case I needed help. Many times, an elder would press a note of encouragement into my hand as he passed the offering plate. Our church auditorium had three main aisles. An elder would walk those aisles before and after the service, watching and waiting. If he sensed I was in trouble or caught in a draining conversation, he would swoop in, take me by the arm, and say, "Excuse us, please. Mary is needed elsewhere." I was then ushered to my car, hugged, and told, "We are praying for you. We love you. Go home." It was amazing! These kind acts served as not only an important factor in my recovery, but a living example of God's comfort and compassion at work in my life.

Looking back, I realize many of these men who so freely and faithfully encouraged me had endured great pain in their own lives. They had experienced the compassion and comfort of God and were quick to share it with me. Now that I am on the other side of that pit, I am motivated to encourage others as a link in God's circle of encouragement.

You have heard the old saying, "What goes around, comes around." Truer words were never spoken when talking about comfort and encouragement. We all need the love and comfort of God, especially during tough times. Those tough times can come in all shapes, sizes, and forms and can vary from person to person. For example, we have one child who has been known to run an extremely high fever, walk around on a broken foot, and have a headache that would put me in bed—all without a word of complaint. The doctors have always been amazed at this child's *high* tolerance for pain. We have another child who has been known to dissolve into hysterics at the sight of a splinter embedded in a finger and to turn ghastly pale and almost faint at the antiseptic smell when opening the door of the doctor's office. The doctors have been amazed at this child's *low* tolerance for pain. The difference between the two does not reflect a right or wrong reaction. It is what it is. When each child is in pain, they both need understanding and comfort. God offers His encouragement to us, no matter how minor the pain may seem to others. If it is important to us, it is important to Him. In the same way, we need to share the comfort He has given us.

What about you, girlfriend? Do you long for someone who will offer you a word of encouragement? Does your broken heart cry out for compassion? Do you need something for your pain? Come to the God of all comfort. He is always there for you.

Let's Pray

Father, I am amazed at how You love me through others. Your compassion heals and encourages me and is a gift of love from Your heart to my life. Help me receive that gift and then give it away to someone else in need. I want to be Your hands and feet to those around me who are hurting. Give me eyes to see them, Lord. In Jesus's name, amen.

The Faithful God

El Hanne'eman

Gwen Smith

Today's Truth

Know therefore that the LORD your God is God; he is the faithful God, keeping his covenant of love to a thousand generations of those who love him and keep his commands. (Deuteronomy 7:9)

Friend to Friend

I was on my way home from running errands. As I approached our neighborhood, my cell phone rang. The call was from my tween-age daughter.

"Hi, Mom. It's Kennedy. Where are you?"

"Hey, baby! I ran some errands and will be home in just a few minutes. What's up?"

"Well, I wanted to see if you and I could go shopping for a new bathing suit this afternoon, and—don't say *no*—I'd like to get a feather in my hair. Can we, Mom?"

Oh. No. She. Didn't!

I was taken aback by the bold expectations of my daughter. *Don't say no?* I thought. *Really? C'mon, girl. I'm the parent. You're the child. Get a grip.*

What I said to her was, "Honey, we are several weeks away from swim season. I'm not sure that today is a good day for all of this. And by the way, you're free to share your heart with me and to tell me your desires, but you do not get to tell me what I can and can't say no to. I'm pulling into the neighborhood now and will see you in a minute."

Later, as I considered her angle—the way she positioned her request—my heart leaped with conviction. How often do I approach God with a request wrapped up in a demand that He's not to tell me *no*?

Jesus told His disciples they could ask for anything. He even said that when we ask in His name, what we ask for would be given to us.

> I tell you the truth, anyone who has faith in me will do what I have been doing. He will do even greater things than these, because I am going to the Father. And I will do whatever you ask in my name, so that the Son may bring glory to the Father. You may ask me for anything in my name, and I will do it. (John 14:12–14)

Let's consider the context here. When Jesus said "You may ask me for anything," it wasn't an open invitation for the will of man to reign. It was an invitation for man to participate in the will of God through prayer. It was about us asking for things that will bring glory to God the Father. Asking "in my name" is all about the will of God being done on earth as it is in heaven—not the whim of mankind.

Then what about the "name it and claim it" theology? Is God obligated to answer our prayers in the way we want Him to? No, He's not. Does God want you to have a million-dollar home and drive a Hummer? Not sure. Does God want you to be healed of that diagnosis, disease, or physical challenge? Possibly. I don't know His exact plan for your life. What I do know is this: God is a good and faithful God. "The works of his hands are faithful and just; all his precepts are trustworthy. They are steadfast for ever and ever, done in faithfulness and uprightness" (Psalm 111:7–8).

All throughout Scripture we see that God is faithful. The Hebrew name for the faithful God is El Hanne'eman. This name of God first appears in Deuteronomy 7:9: "Know therefore that the LORD your God is God; he is the faithful God, keeping his covenant of love to a thousand generations of those who love him and keep his commands." When it comes to God's character, faithfulness doesn't mean that He will always come through for us in the way we expect. It means He will see His plans through to completion, that He will keep His promises, that He will continue to work in our lives for our ultimate good—not necessarily our immediate happiness.

If we think that God can't say no to us, then we've put *ourselves* on the throne and not God. Prayer is not about getting God to do what we want Him to do; it is about releasing God's will on earth as it is in heaven (Matthew 6:10). It doesn't change His mind, and He's not a genie in a bottle for whom our wish is His command. God is God—and He is faithful, no matter which way He moves.

I love my daughter. I mean, I really, really, really love my daughter. But just because she asks me for something doesn't mean that I'm going to grant her request. I love her too much for that. God is our heavenly Father. Our Parent. The Faithful One. He wants mature, wise children. Not spoiled children. He loves us too much for that.

He even told His own Son *no* in order to accomplish His great purposes. On the night He was betrayed, Jesus was distraught to the point of sweating blood in the Garden of Gethsemane. Crying out to God, He "knelt down and prayed, saying, 'Father, if you are willing, remove this cup from me. Nevertheless, not my will, but yours, be done'" (Luke 22:41–42, ESV).

God said no to Jesus because the request of His Son did not line up with His will. And because God said no, you and I can experience grace, forgiveness, peace, and salvation. In order for God to be glorified in His life, Jesus had to submit to the will of the Father. In order for God to be glorified in our lives, we too must submit to the will of the Father—and His will is always what's best for us because He is faithful.

Coming to terms with this truth is tough, no doubt about that. At times the wounds of life leave us reeling. At times God allows trials and temptations that seem unbearable. Even in those times, God remains the same and He can be trusted. It's a choice we have to make. And that choice is directly linked with the promise of blessing. Psalm 84:12 says, "O LORD Almighty, blessed is the man who trusts in you."

God's names reflect His character, and He is El Hanne'eman—the Faithful God. So no matter what you pray for or desire, you can trust Him, whether His answer is no or yes.

Let's Pray

Dear Lord, the Faithful God, El Hanne'eman, You are my Father and I know that You have a plan for me. Please bind me to Your will, and teach me to desire Your heart above all else. Help me to hold unswervingly to the hope that I profess, because You who promised are faithful (Hebrews 10:23). In Jesus's name, amen.

Day 4

The God of Love

Mary Southerland

Today's Truth

And so we know and rely on the love God has for us. God is love. (1 John 4:16)

Friend to Friend

It had been a wonderful day. We were all tired after hiking Grandfather Mountain and stopping to picnic beside a pristine North Carolina creek on the way back to our little vacation cabin. Bedtime preparation was proceeding amazingly well. All that mountain air and country cooking was a natural sedative for our two pleasantly exhausted children. I looked forward to joining my husband, Dan, in the front porch swing to cuddle, gaze at the stars, and dream of what might be.

Soon Danna, our three-year-old daughter, was out like a light—one down and one to go. Jered, our six-year-old son, scrambled into bed, ready to recap the hiking adventure and make a plan for tomorrow. We snuggled under the fluffy down comforter, talking and laughing about how much fun the day had been. Then we settled into a cozy, comfortable silence.

His question ripped through the quiet room and through my heart, exposing every fear and insecurity carefully hidden there: "Why didn't she want me?"

I immediately knew what he meant. After years of trying to have children naturally, Dan and I discovered that God had a wonderfully different plan for us. We adopted both Jered and Danna as infants and marveled daily at the precious gift of our two children. For years, I had known this question was inevitable, but I was still caught off guard by Jered's probing words. My uncertain heart cried out to my Father. I needed an answer—for Jered and for me. Instantly, it came. Bruno!

When Jered was four years old, we were given a chocolate-colored Labrador puppy that quickly outgrew our small yard, our not-so-understanding neighbors, and our apprehensive children. We named this gentle canine giant Bruno.

With each passing day, Bruno became an increasingly frustrated dog. Our postage-stamp-sized backyard offered little room for him to romp and run freely. Our elderly neighbors did not appreciate his early morning barking alarm, and our kids soon refused to venture into the backyard because Bruno, who loved them and wanted to play, delighted in pinning them to the ground with his massive paws while covering their faces with slobbery kisses. Before long, it became clear to all of us that we were not the right family for Bruno.

After an intensive search, we discovered Adopt-a-Pet, a remarkable organization that finds homes for animals whose owners, for one reason or another, cannot keep them. We were promised Bruno would be placed in just the right home where he would be loved, well cared for, and would have plenty of room to run and play. For weeks, we talked and explained, struggling our way to the difficult decision that it was time to put Bruno up for adoption. Still, on the day they came to pick him up, we all cried. Yes, we knew it was the best plan for Bruno, for us, and for a very excited family that wanted a Labrador, but it still hurt. Sometimes, doing the right thing—the best thing, the highest thing—is also the most painful thing.

As I looked into the beautiful blue eyes of the little boy I loved more than life itself, I prayed for just the right words. "Jered, do you remember Bruno?"

At the memory of the dog, Jered smiled and sadly whispered, "I still miss him."

I nodded in agreement and replied, "I know, son. It's okay for you to still miss him. I know you loved Bruno and were sad when we had to give him away. But do you remember *why* we gave Bruno away?"

Jered thought for a moment and carefully answered, "Because we loved him so much and we knew we couldn't take care of him right...and because he wasn't very happy...and because we wanted the best home in the whole wide world for him." He looked up at me and smiled, satisfied that he had covered all the bases.

I paused for a moment, basking in the simple and faithful wisdom of my Father, spoken through the heart of my only son. Now I was ready to answer his unsettling question. "She *did* want you, honey. And she *did* love you—so much, in fact, that she was willing to give you away, just like we gave Bruno away. Just as we wanted what was best for Bruno, your birth mother wanted what was best for *you*." I fully recognize that it was an extremely simplistic illustration for a profoundly complex life circumstance, but it was enough for Jered at that moment.

I lay there in the darkness, holding this chosen baby in my arms, listening to him breathe as he drifted into a peaceful, trust-filled sleep. My heart filled with wonder and awe at the faultless plan and complete provision of God in our lives. With tears of gratitude spilling down my face, I thanked God for two courageous birth mothers, for the plan of adoption that brought our children to us, and for God's perfect work through an unusual servant named Bruno. With a contented smile on his face, Jered sighed, turned over, and whispered the most precious words a mother can hear: "I love you, Mom."

We are all desperate to be loved and to love. We search for significance and are created with the innate need to belong. Sadly, we sometimes pursue worth in worthless places. We demand validation from invalid sources—until we finally realize that the only place we can find true love—agape love—is in the One who is love, God. *Agape* is a Greek word for *love* and is beautifully described by John, who wrote, "And so we know and rely on the love God has for us. *God is love.* Whoever lives in love lives in God, and God in him" (1 John 4:16). God has adopted you into His family because He loves you. He is your Father. You are chosen and dearly loved. Created by God, for God.

In the darkness of that mountain cabin, I caught a new perspective of God's stubborn love and the absolutely unthinkable sacrifice He made by giving up His one and only Son, Jesus Christ, for me and for you. It is only through a personal relationship with Him that we experience authentic love, a love that displaces thoughts of rejection and banishes feelings of abandonment. It is in this priceless gift that we comprehend the amazing truth that even if we were never wanted or planned by human heart and mind, we were planned and wanted in the heart and mind of God! And that, dear friend, is more than enough!

For God so loved the world that he gave his
one and only Son, that whoever believes in
him shall not perish but have eternal life.
(John 3:16)

Let's Pray

Thank You for loving me, God. Honestly, I don't understand the kind of love that sent Jesus Christ to the cross so that I can live. But today I celebrate Your love. Help me to remember that I am chosen and because of Your love, I will never be alone or abandoned. You created me for a personal relationship with You. I am not an accident and I am not a mistake. I was created in response to Your plan. Today, I celebrate the fact that I am a chosen child of the King. In Jesus's name, amen.

The Lord Our Righteousness
Yahweh Tsidkenu

Mary Southerland

Today's Truth

"Behold, the days are coming," declares the Lord, "when I will raise up for David a righteous Branch; and He will reign as king and act wisely and do justice and righteousness in the land. In His days Judah will be saved, and Israel will dwell securely; and this is His name by which He will be called, '*The LORD our righteousness.*'" (Jeremiah 23:5–6, NASB)

Friend to Friend

On a recent flight, I was thumbing through a magazine when the title of an article caught my eye. "Image is everything," the author declared. For a few seconds, I found myself mentally agreeing with the author's statement until I recognized the subtle lie hidden in the seemingly benign words.

As followers of God, we sometimes focus on presenting the right image while neglecting the spiritual discipline of integrity.

Our public lives are only as authentic as our private lives. We can say that we are fully devoted followers of God, but if who or what we are at home, in our relationships, and in our daily walk does not reflect Him and His principles, we are not living authentic lives. Image really is nothing without integrity to back it up. Image is who and what people *think* we are, while integrity is who and what we *really* are. Billy Graham once said, "Integrity is the glue that holds our way of life together. We must constantly strive to keep our integrity intact. When wealth is lost, nothing is lost; when health is lost, something is lost; when character is lost, all is lost."[44]

Bobby Jones was one of the greatest golfers to ever compete, having won all four major tournaments in the United States and Britain in 1930. Early in his career, Jones made it to the final play-off in the US Open. While he was setting up a fairly difficult shot, his golf club accidentally touched the ball. Jones became angry, turned to the marshals, and admitted the error. Since the marshals hadn't seen the ball move, they left the decision to Jones. It was a two-stroke penalty, which Bobby immediately called on himself, not knowing he would later lose the tournament by a single stroke.

Bobby dismissed praise for his honesty by replying, "You might as well praise a man for *not* robbing a bank." Jones may have lost the tournament, but his character is legendary. Today, the United States Golf Association's award for sportsmanship is known as the Bobby Jones Award.

I have heard it said that integrity is what you do when no one is watching or that character is best illustrated by how you treat people who can do absolutely nothing for you. Integrity is a heart issue. To have integrity—to live an integrated life—means that what we believe, what we think, what we say, and what we do are all consistent.

We develop integrity as a spiritual habit by deciding beforehand to do the right thing.

Integrity matters to God because He is holy and righteous. Matthew 5:8 says, "Blessed are the pure in heart, for they will see God." The Greek word translated as "pure" means "ready for sacrifice." In other words, the choices we make should be living sacrifices, holy and acceptable to God as acts of worship. Romans 12:1 says, "Therefore, I urge you, brothers, in view of God's mercy, to offer your bodies as living sacrifices, holy and pleasing to God—this is your spiritual act of worship."

Sadly, many of us have bought into the lie that the rules, the commandments of God, do not necessarily apply to us. Certainly this was an issue in the days of the prophet Jeremiah, who lived during the destruction of Judah and was constantly calling the people and kings of Judah to repent and live righteous lives. According to Jeremiah, the designated priests and overseers were not taking care of their flocks. Jeremiah rebuked the authority figures who were supposed to care for their sheep and confronted them with the truth that, because of the shepherds' neglect, only a remnant of faithful people were left. But God promised to replace the failed shepherds with new ones who would lead the people in the paths of righteousness. Eventually, God would even provide the ultimate King, the ultimate Shepherd—Jesus Christ—to lead His people in His ways and in the paths of righteousness.

> "Behold, the days are coming," declares the Lord,
> "When I will raise up for David a righteous Branch;
> And He will reign as king and act wisely
> And do justice and righteousness in the land.

"In His days Judah will be saved,
And Israel will dwell securely;
And this is His name by which He will be called,
'The LORD our righteousness'" [Yahweh Tsidkenu].
(Jeremiah 23:5–6, NASB)

Tsidkenu literally means "still or straight" and refers to a standard of measurement. Our sinful natures are measured against God's holy nature. The source of all righteousness is Yahweh. He alone is perfect and righteous. Any goodness, any integrity we have, comes from Him. Yahweh Tsidkenu, in His great love and mercy, knowing we are hopeless and helpless, extended His grace to redeem us from our lost state and bring us into a personal relationship with Him—a relationship that does not expect perfection but does expect the pursuit of the perfect God.

At the close of the sermon, a church member came forward to speak with the pastor. He was upset, convicted of his blatant disobedience to God. With tears streaming down his face, the repentant man took the pastor's hand to confess that his life was full of sin, but what came out was, "My sin is full of life." I can relate.

I am always amused but also saddened by people who think that just because I am in full-time ministry, I must be holier than they are, better than they are, or don't have to battle sin like they do. Just ask my husband and children or anyone who knows me. They will blow that theory right out of the water. Seriously! As long as I live in this fallen world and sport this frail humanity, I will struggle with sin.

However, I have refined several tactics for camouflaging my sinful nature. Rationalization is a personal favorite. And there is always the handy comparison ploy, measuring my sin against the sin of another. At times, I subscribe to the popular "bury it and hope it will go away" tactic.

The reality, of course, is that nothing satisfies the payment that sin demands except the blood of Jesus Christ, along with my response to His sacrifice in true, unadulterated repentance, on my face before my Holy God who made a way for me to know Him.

When we turn our lives over to God, He sets our feet on the right path—the path of His righteousness, not ours. To stay on that path requires continual choices to avoid sin. Instead, we tend to take side trips, create detours, and wind up on the wrong road headed in the wrong direction.

Solomon warned us to stay away from evil paths. "Don't turn off the road of goodness; keep away from evil paths" (Proverbs 4:27, NCV). "Keep away" literally means "to turn aside or drag from." In other words, when we see sin or even the opportunity to sin, we should turn around and run in the opposite direction. We should "drag ourselves" away from sin. What do we do instead? We flirt with sin. We want to be delivered from temptation but would really like to keep in touch. We pray for God to "lead us not into temptation" and then deliberately place ourselves in its path. In our arrogance, we think we can handle sin and temptation on our own. That very attitude is an open invitation for the Enemy, daring him to take his best shot.

There is no holding pattern for believers, nor can we live in a neutral state. We are either going forward or backward. We are either being renewed or consumed. Girlfriend, do not relinquish any more life territory to the Enemy. Run from sin—straight into the arms of your holy and righteous God. He's got you covered with His righteousness. He is your Yahweh Tsidkenu.

Let's Pray

Father, I come to You right now, asking You to examine my heart and show me every impurity hidden there. Search my desires and thoughts, and show me the disobedience that breaks Your heart and hinders my walk with You. I want to please You with every choice and decision I make. Forgive me for the hypocrisy in my life. I lay down my pride and my agenda and choose instead to seek and follow You. In Jesus's name, amen.

Phillipians – 2:14
Do everything without grumbling or questioning that you may be blameless + innocent, children of God without blemish in the midst of a crooked + perverse generation, among whom you shine like lights of the world

Now It's Your Turn

Time for Reflection

- The word *father* can stir up a whole spectrum of emotions. For some of us, they are sweet; for others, sour. Thankfully, regardless of our experience with earthly fathers, the Lord is our Abba, Father. Perfect in love: gentle, patient, and kind. Look up these verses, and note what is written about being a child of God.

  Romans 8:15–17 ____________________

  2 Corinthians 6:18 ____________________

  1 John 3:1 ____________________

  Philippians 2:14–15 ____________________

- What do you imagine are a few of the differences between the actions and emotions of an orphan and those of a child of a king?

  Orphan: ____________________

  Child of a king: ____________________

  Which most closely mirrors your life?

- What do you think are a few characteristics of a perfect father? List some on the lines below.

  Loving, caring, strong, smart, Godly, strict, faithful, generous, patient

  All done? Now circle the ones you have experienced in God. What conclusions can you draw?

- This week, one of the devotions featured God as our Comfort. Describe a recent time when you received and/or gave encouragement or comfort. What were the results?

- God is also El Hanne'eman, the Faithful One. Hebrews 10:23 says, "Let us hold unswervingly to the hope we profess, for he who promised is faithful." What hope does this verse encourage us to hold unswervingly to as we remember God's faithfulness? (Read verses 19–22 if you need a clue.)

- Respond out loud with a statement of intention. Fill in the blank to make Hebrews 10:23 personal: "Today I am choosing to hold unswervingly to hope when it comes to ____________________ ________________ because I have committed this burden to God and I know that He is faithful."

- God is faithful even when we are not. We all fail and have selfish tendencies. In spite of our wandering ways, God remains steadfast. Read and discuss the following verse: "If we are faithless, he will remain faithful, for he cannot disown himself" (2 Timothy 2:13).

  How does this verse encourage you? Have you been praying for the Lord to answer according to His will or according to yours? (Peel back a few layers here and be transparent, keeping in mind that there is no condemnation in Christ.)

- Mary shared a tender story this week about a conversation with her young son about his adoption. Love led the dialogue and gave divine answers to complicated heart questions. Her son's confidence and sense of significance gained traction that day. Write three words that describe how you feel about your significance.

  ____________, ____________, ____________

- Knowing that God is love and that His love for you is perfect, do your three words line up with the words God would use to define your significance? Identify one step that you can take in order to see yourself through the eyes of God.
- God is Yahweh Tsidkenu, the Lord Our Righteousness. Read Psalm 51:10 and fill in the blanks: "Create in me a ____________ ____________, O God, and ____________ a ____________ ____________ within me."

  Contemplate and discuss the benefits that a clean heart and a renewed spirit bring to your life...to your family...to your relationships...and to your choices.
- Wrap up your response time with prayer. Move from confession, to adoration, to thanksgiving, and end with your petitions (personal prayer needs).

Going Deeper with God

List: the names of God and their meanings that were covered in the devotions this week.

1. ________________________________
2. ________________________________
3. ________________________________

4. ____
5. ____

Read: 1 John.

Deepen: Search your Bible for seven verses that talk about the love of God. Begin by reading Psalm 139. Write each verse on an index card. Memorize one verse a day for the next seven days, and share each verse with someone you love.

Reach out: Write a note of encouragement or comfort to someone in need. Let them know you are praying for them. If you can, offer to take care of a specific need such as preparing a meal, dropping by the grocery store, or picking up their dry cleaning. Look for a need and meet it.

Your GiG *Knowing God by Name* Journal

Spend a few moments contemplating and journaling about some of the scriptural truths that moved your heart as you read the devotions this week. Then use the space below to collect your thoughts or write a prayer of response to God.

____

____

____

____

____

____

____

Know therefore that the LORD your God is God; he is the faithful God, keeping his covenant of love to a thousand generations of those who love him and keep his commands. (Deuteronomy 7:9)

Day 1

The God of Glory
El Kahvohd

Sharon Jaynes

Today's Truth

The voice of the Lord is over the waters; the God of glory thunders, the Lord thunders over the mighty waters. (Psalm 29:3)

Friend to Friend

The sun had not pried open the day quite yet. My husband and I had been traveling with some friends for several days, going from one Pacific island to another. While I had enjoyed seeing God's creation, I had missed our times alone—just the two of us, me and God.

Wrapped in a blanket and with a hot cup of coffee in hand, I snuck away with my Beloved for a quiet rendezvous before others in the house stirred. As I gazed out through sliding-glass doors, I drank in the view of the stilled Pacific Ocean spread before me. All seemed gray in this predawn expanse of sky and sea.

When I grabbed my Bible, it fell open to the middle. I didn't bother to turn the pages. I looked down and read familiar words from the well-worn love letter: "May God be gracious to us and bless us and make his face shine upon us" (Psalm 67:1). When I looked up, I noticed the sun struggling to send its rays through two small openings in the early morning clouds…two holes side by side, like headlights on high beam. As I continued watching the morning sun stretch its arms of light, another break in the clouds provided a slit for the rays to escape. An upturned crescent emerged directly under the two circular beams above. And then I saw it—a celestial smiley face beaming through the clouds. Divine delight, a holy grin! God's radiant smile welcomed me to another day.

I had a front row seat in God's theater as His glory pierced the darkness and spilled forth grace that filled my heart. While I rose to pursue Him, He had beaten me to the punch and reminded me that He was the one pursuing me. I simply showed up. Ah, sometimes we simply need to show up, to turn aside and see His glory on display. Our God is infinitely powerful and intimately personal.

God had made His "face to shine upon me," and my smile, be it ever so small and unassuming, mirrored His gift to me. As if the words in His love letter weren't enough, He wrote a message to me in the sky like a love-struck beau. His passionate pursuit amazed me, and I was drawn like a moth to the flame of His love. Me—the bride pursued.

Months later, I told a friend about the precious moment God and I shared on that small Pacific island so far away from home.

"Things like that never happen to me," she sighed.

"Oh yes, they do," I assured her. "You just need to learn how to recognize them."

And I believe that with my whole heart. God has pulled out all the stops to reveal glimpses of His glory. But many, I dare say most, don't see it, don't hear it, and don't taste it. Jesus knew the difference it would make for our souls to be alert to moments of sudden glory when God makes His presence known: "Blessed are your eyes because they see," Jesus said, "and your ears because they hear" (Matthew 13:16).

The word *glory* is a weighty word. It seems so otherworldly. We can catch glimpses of its meaning throughout Scripture, but then like a shooting star that appears for just a moment, it quickly slips away in the vast expanse of God's infinite wisdom. But if you remember from Day 1 of Week 1, glory is how God makes His presence known.

In the Old Testament, the most common Hebrew word for "glory" is *kabod,* meaning "weight, honor, or esteem."[45] It refers to God's splendor and majesty. He made Himself known through a fire, a cloud, handwriting on a wall, a still small voice, a parting sea, and a tumbling Jericho wall, just to mention a few.

In the New Testament, the Greek word for "glory" is *doxa.* John wrote, "The Word became flesh and made his dwelling among us. We have seen his *glory,* the *glory* of the One and Only, who came from the Father, full of grace and truth" (John 1:14). In Hebrews 1:3, the writer reveals this about Jesus: "The Son is the radiance of God's *glory* and the exact representation of his being, sustaining all things by his powerful word." God made His presence known through Jesus. He said to Philip, "Anyone who has seen me has seen the Father" (John 14:9).

The Greek verb form of *glory,* translated "to glorify," is *doxazo,* and primarily means "to magnify, extol, praise, to ascribe honor to God, acknowledging Him as to His being, attributes and acts"[46]—in other words, His glory. When you glorify God, you are giving a display or manifestation—or a reflection—of His character. To magnify God is to make Him easy to see.

God's glory is how He makes Himself known. He is the God of

glory, and He makes Himself known through nature, the Bible, circumstances, and people like you and me. When we open our eyes and tune our ears to the timbre of God's voice, we will experience His glory, the manifestation of His presence, in our lives on a daily basis.

Can you remember a time when you sensed God's presence and you were absolutely sure it was Him? Perhaps it was when you first believed, or maybe it happened just yesterday. You may have felt an overwhelming sense of His love, received an answer to prayer, felt an inexplicable peace, or witnessed a miracle. But when it happened… oh, when it happened…you knew you had encountered the Divine. The moment came and went, and you were awestruck. Do you remember it? That was God making Himself known to you personally. I call that *a sudden glory*—an intimate moment with your Creator, the lover of your soul, a glimpse of heaven.[47]

Oh, sister, our God is not aloof. He does not sit on His throne and merely watch His image-bearers flit about in the blur of life. No, He makes His presence known. He sends you love notes all day long. Holy Post-It notes lavished freely. He is the God of glory who makes His presence known through the beauty of a sunset, the sweetness of a kiss, the laughter of a child, the fierceness of a thunderclap, the gentleness of a breeze.

Solomon reminds us that God "has planted eternity in the human heart" (Ecclesiastes 3:11, NLT). Every person has an ache, a knowing, that there has to be something more than this life. And while that ache will never go away until we leave this earthly home and inhale eternity, the God of glory gives us glimpses of heaven as He makes His presence known through moments of sudden glory just waiting to be discovered.

Today, I encourage you to open your eyes, tune your ears, and alert your senses to moments of sudden glory as God passionately pursues your heart and relentlessly romances your soul—as the God of glory makes His majestic presence and intimate wooing known to you.

Let's Pray

God of glory, majestic is Your name in all the earth. Your glory is too difficult for me to understand, imagine, or conceive. And yet You give me glimpses of Your glory all around. I sit with the blind beggar, face upturned. "What do you want?" Jesus asked. "Lord, I want to see." Oh, God, that is what I want as well. I want to see. I want to see glimpses of Your glory in all of life. Help me not to miss them. In Jesus's name, amen.

My Portion

Chelqi

Gwen Smith

Today's Truth

"The Lord is my portion," says my soul, "therefore I will hope in him." (Lamentations 3:24, ESV)

Friend to Friend

I am a lot of things, but low maintenance is not one of them. Straight up, I am a girl with some constant cravings. Though I do try to savor life moments with gratitude, I fail all the time. Many days, I find myself looking beyond my now to my next, driven by longing and discontent. I seek God's blessings instead of seeking God. I seek His hand instead of His heart. This frazzles my peace and messes with my joy. It tangles my heart in knots until I begin to slouch through my days to the tune of "I Can't Get No Satisfaction"!

I sometimes run to God as if He's a celestial Wal-Mart purposed to satisfy my every want. *Change my family. Fix my job problem, God. Do it my way!* Instead of leaning in to hear the whispered will of the Lord, I selfishly shout my will, my desires, and my demands. *Lord, give me relief from life pressures,* I insist, when I should be asking Him for strength to endure them. In my desperate race to fill my megasized heart-cart with things that I want, I rob myself of what really matters: the pursuit of God and the blessings found in Him alone.

The truth is that even us Jesus girls—you know, *good* Christian women who strive each day to live for Christ—continually sin and wallow in the shallow, unsatisfying waters of discontentment. We tell God what we'd like Him to do for us so we can be happy and then expect Him to intervene in ways that suit us. We blur the lines between our wants and our needs, between *our* plans and *God's* plans.

Does God need us to tell Him how to be God? Isn't that what we do when we stomp our feet before His throne and whine about all the things that need fixing instead of praising Him for the strength He graciously gives us to get through? While we're certainly encouraged by Scripture to make our requests known to the Father (Philippians 4:6), the highest calling on our lives is to love God with all our hearts, souls, bodies, and minds (Matthew 22:37). We can do both, but we are commanded to seek God first: to look to Him as our Ultimate. Our Portion.

David modeled this beautifully when he called out to God in the midst of trouble and recognized Him as being enough: "I cry to you, O Lord; I say, 'You are my refuge, my portion in the land of the living'" (Psalm 142:5). In Psalm 119, the psalmist recognizes God as his portion and takes surrender a step further by tethering his satisfaction with obedience. "You are my portion, O Lord; I have promised to obey your words. I have sought your face with all my heart; be gracious to me according to your promise" (verses 57–58).

Life is unpredictable. There will always be days that we want to yell, *C'mon, God! Throw me a bone here! I could use a little help, please!* It is not a bad thing to call to God in the midst of our struggles. In fact, we should! The big game changer, however, is seeking not God's presents, but His presence. Refuge from our circumstances and contentment in the midst of them is found in the center of our surrender.

Asaph wrote Psalm 73 with a lot on his mind. He was flustered about all the bad people surrounding him. He wondered why God wasn't smacking them around for being so wretched. Then his woes turned to worship as he entered into the sanctuary of God (verse 17). His heart began to untangle when he remembered God's sovereignty. In verse 26, he finally landed in a good place: "My flesh and my heart may fail, but God is the strength of my heart and my portion forever."

He took a deep breath and found his God-confidence.

Oh, how I can relate to that!

The Bible shows us time and time again that when we prioritize God—when we look to Him to be our Portion, or Chelqi[48]—we are supernaturally equipped to rest in Him. Do you remember that old hymn "His Eye Is on the Sparrow"? Girlfriend, God sees it all. He knows what's going on. As Jesus reminded His listeners during the Sermon on the Mount, if divine eyes rest on tiny sparrows and flowers of the fields, how much more are the needs and desires of God's children known to Him?

The Message paraphrase of the Bible says it like this:

> If God gives such attention to the appearance of wildflowers—most of which are never even seen—don't you think he'll attend to you, take pride in you, do his best for you? What I'm trying to do here is to get you to relax, to not be so preoccupied with *getting,* so you can respond to God's *giving.* People who don't know God and the way he works

> fuss over these things, but you know both God and how he works. Steep your life in God-reality, God-initiative, and God-provisions. Don't worry about missing out. You'll find all your everyday human concerns will be met.
>
> Give your entire attention to what God is doing right now, and don't get worked up about what may or may not happen tomorrow. God will help you deal with whatever hard things come up when the time comes. (Matthew 6:30–34)

So what's the connection point between our longings and His provision? Perhaps the better question is not *what* but *who*? Pastor and theologian Charles Spurgeon said it this way:

> It is not "The Lord is *partly* my portion," nor "The Lord is *in* my portion"; but he himself makes up the sum total of my soul's inheritance. Within the circumference of that circle lies all that we possess or desire. The *Lord* is my portion. Not his grace merely, nor his love, nor his covenant, but Jehovah himself.[49]

Once again, Spurgeon hits the nail on the head. We are distracted cravers when we expect people, places, and things to fill our hearts as only God can. God loves us so much. Why do we forget this all the time? His plan is perfect and we can trust Him. He knows our needs and desires. When we seek Him *as* the answer instead of *for* the answer, God enables us to rest in confidence that He's working on our behalf and in our best interest, to bring glory to Himself through our lives.

Set aside your list of wants today, and seek God. Go before Him with a heart of worship and adoration. Get lost in His presence. Remember His mercy. Relish His grace. Love Him. Seek Him. Choose Him as your Portion.

Let's Pray

Dear Lord, my Portion, You are all I need. Please forgive me for the times when I seek Your blessings before I seek Your heart. Help me to trust Your plan and rest in Your grace. In Jesus's name, amen.

The Living God

El Chay

Sharon Jaynes

Today's Truth

And Hezekiah prayed to the LORD: "O LORD, God of Israel, enthroned between the cherubim, you alone are God over all the kingdoms of the earth. You have made heaven and earth. Give ear, O LORD, and hear; open your eyes, O LORD, and see; listen to the words Sennacherib has sent to insult the *living God*." (2 Kings 19:15–16)

Friend to Friend

Howard was rich—very rich. His father made a fortune by designing a drill bit that could bore through hard rock, allowing oil drillers to reach large pockets of previously inaccessible oil. His tool company held the patent for the new drill bit, manufactured the bit, and leased it to oil companies who used it.

All through his childhood, Howard struggled in conventional schools. A loner with few friends, he preferred to learn by tinkering with mechanical things. When his mother forbade him to buy a motorcycle, he built a motor and attached it to his bicycle. Problem solved.

When Howard was still a teenager, both of his parents passed away, leaving him a substantial estate. At age nineteen, Howard moved to Hollywood where he tried his hand at movie making with great success. Then in the mid-1930s, he redirected his obsession toward aviation. He bought several airplanes, hired numerous engineers and designers, and was determined to make faster, sleeker, better planes. In 1944, Howard's company designed a large flying boat intended to carry both people and supplies to the war in Europe. The *Spruce Goose,* the largest plane ever constructed, was flown once in 1947 and then never flew again.

Howard was a billionaire when the idea of a millionaire was beyond the comprehension of ordinary people. While he was very successful in the world's eyes, it was the "world's eye" that he wanted to avoid. Eventually he withdrew altogether from human contact, moved into Las Vegas's Desert Inn hotel, and rarely left his suite. When the hotel threatened to evict him, he bought the entire establishment and then proceeded to buy up multiple Las Vegas properties to extend his perimeter of control. For the next several years, not a single person laid eyes on the billionaire hermit.

Howard spent the rest of his life trying to avoid germs. His obsessive-compulsive behavior caused him to lay naked in bed in darkened hotel rooms in what he considered a germ-free zone. When he died in 1976 from heart failure, his six-foot-four-inch, ninety-pound frame was covered in filth, his hair and beard were tangled and rancid, and his fingernails looked like claws. He had become such a hermit in his last years that no one was really sure it was him. The Treasury Department had to use fingerprints to confirm that the deceased man was indeed the billionaire Howard Hughes.

The story of Howard Hughes screams a warning to us all. The false gods of a materialistic culture will not lead to true happiness and joy in this life. They are mere "things," with no more power than the golden calf the Israelites once worshiped. It is easy to look at Hughes's life and feel pretty good about yourself. But, friend, I fear the materialistic cravings of our self-centered culture are really no different than his.

We fall into the trap of idolatry when we falsely believe that anything other than God will satisfy our deepest longings. When we think that "just a little bit more" will soothe the ache, when we feel the right relationship will fill the void, when we believe that we need anything or anyone to be truly happy, we place a false idol on the throne of our soul. It is only through a personal relationship with the living God, El Chay, that you or I will experience abundant life on earth and eternal life thereafter.

King Hezekiah introduces us to the name El Chay in 2 Kings 17. One day he received a bad piece of mail. You know the kind. The biopsy is positive. The power bill is past due. The application is denied. The kind of mail that makes you want to scribble "Return to Sender" across the top and pretend it never came.

The letter was from Sennacherib, the king of Assyria, who had crushed forty-six towns in Judah and carried off tens of thousands captive. And now, Sennacherib was coming after Jerusalem and King Hezekiah's people. And even though Hezekiah had rebuilt and fortified the city walls, produced a massive battery of weapons, created a tunnel to bring water into the city and ensure their supply would not be cut off—even though he was prepared for war—he was not foolish enough to depend on human strength and ingenuity for victory. He called out to El Chay, the Living God, for their defense.

> Hezekiah received the letter from the messengers and
> read it. Then he went up to the temple of the Lord and

> spread it out before the LORD. And Hezekiah prayed to the LORD: "O LORD, God of Israel, enthroned between the cherubim, you alone are God over all the kingdoms of the earth. You have made heaven and earth. Give ear, O LORD, and hear; open your eyes, O LORD, and see; listen to the words Sennacherib has sent to insult the *living God.*
>
> "It is true, O LORD, that the Assyrian kings have laid waste these nations and their lands. They have thrown their gods into the fire and destroyed them, for they were not gods but only wood and stone, fashioned by men's hands. Now, O LORD our God, deliver us from his hand, so that all kingdoms on earth may know that you alone, O LORD, are God." (2 Kings 19:14–19)

Hezekiah recognized the powerlessness of the lifeless pagan gods made of wood, stone, and precious metal. And he knew the unstoppable power of the living God who created all three. So he prayed and he trusted.

> That night the angel of the LORD went out and put to death a hundred and eighty-five thousand men in the Assyrian camp. When the people got up the next morning—there were all the dead bodies! So Sennacherib king of Assyria broke camp and withdrew. He returned to Nineveh *and stayed there.* (verses 35–36)

I'll bet he did. He stayed put and never mocked the living God or threatened His people again.

When God gave the Ten Commandments, He began with "You shall have no other gods before me" (Exodus 20:3). And yet, all through history we see men and women worshiping false gods, depending on false gods. How silly to think that a golden calf, a wooden pole, or a stone-studded ornament could be a god that protects, prospers, and provides. Silly, right?

And yet the false gods of our world are really no different than the ones of King Hezekiah's day. We live in an idol-infested world, where false gods offer false security to misguided souls. Emotional enemies such as anger, depression, worry, fear, anxiety, addictions, and jealousy are just a few of the Sennacheribs that threaten to take the battering ram and charge the door of our hearts. And what are the idols or false gods that many turn to for comfort? People. Possessions. Position. A fleet of airplanes. A bulging bank account. A prime piece of real estate. We eat. We shop. We place children on the throne. We depend on relationships for love and security. Oh yes, idols abound in our culture.

Howard Hughes discovered just how ineffective the gods of people, possessions, and power can be. He was one of the wealthiest men in history. He was one of the most miserable men in history. His $2.5 billion estate was powerless to help him win the battle he faced every day.

Jesus said, "I have come that they may have life, and have it to the full" (John 10:10). Abundant life. Overflowing life. He said, "I am the way and the truth and the life" (John 14:6).

Let me encourage you today, whatever enemies you face, be they physical, emotional, relational, or spiritual, call out to the living God. Ask Him to drive them out and fill you up. "For he is the living God and he endures forever" (Daniel 6:26).

Let's Pray

O living God, please forgive me for the false gods I have tucked into the recesses of my heart. I know that You are the only One who can fill my empty spaces and mend my broken places. You are El Chay, the Living God who always has been and always will be. You are the God who hears, who sees, and who stands ready to work Your wonders in my life. In Jesus's name, amen.

The Giver of Good Gifts

Mary Southerland

Today's Truth

Every good and perfect gift is from above, coming down from the Father of the heavenly lights, who does not change like shifting shadows. (James 1:17)

Friend to Friend

Our grandchildren are not only a source of great joy in my life, but they are some of my most capable teachers as well. Our three-year-old grandson, Justus, recently reminded me of the profound truth that God is the ultimate gift giver.

Justus loves dirt. If he is not truly dirty, he is not truly happy. One of his favorite toys to play with in his beloved dirt is what he calls a "digger." Justus has quite a collection of diggers. We, along with other family members, his parents, and friends, have happily provided this little hunk of joy with an assortment of plastic dump trucks, bulldozers, backhoes, and excavators. Justus knows the name of each construction vehicle but prefers to call them "diggers," so diggers it is.

Our daughter and son-in-law have wisely allocated a section of their backyard where Justus can happily dig and work and play with all his diggers. He spends hours transferring dirt from one part of his work site to another, creating mounds of dirt while building what he calls "massive" cities and then tearing them down to begin again.

One day, our daughter called to share a precious "Justus story." She was enjoying a beautiful, sunny afternoon in their backyard with Justus and his baby brother, Hudson. Danna was reading and Hudson was snoozing in his bouncy seat while Justus played happily, hard at work with—you guessed it—his diggers. Justus suddenly stopped, sprang to his feet, and thrust both arms in the air as high as he possibly could. With his smiling little face turned toward heaven, Justus shouted at the top of his lungs, "God, thank You for my dirt!"

Time stood still for a moment.

I am almost certain heaven paused as God smiled and replied, *You are so welcome, Justus.* Satisfied, our grandson went back to his digger and dirt project.

And God spoke to my heart.

I tend to forget the goodness of God. But James 1:17 reminds me that God is the ultimate gift giver: "Every good and perfect gift is from above, coming down from the Father of the heavenly lights, who does not change like shifting shadows." How often do I dismiss His gifts, both great and small, as something to which I am somehow entitled? Though I know better, I somehow take His gifts for granted. I just allow my busy schedule to crowd out the wonder of God at work in my life every single day. God used our three-year-old grandson to remind me that God literally fills every minute of every day with gifts from His hand. Why? God wants me to celebrate life—to live a life saturated with His joy.

In biblical times, much like today, times of great joy were often accompanied by the giving of gifts.

> Nehemiah said, "Go and enjoy choice food and sweet drinks, and send some to those who have nothing prepared. This day is sacred to our Lord. Do not grieve, for the joy of the LORD is your strength." (Nehemiah 8:10)

> Mordecai recorded these events, and he sent letters to all the Jews throughout the provinces of King Xerxes, near and far, to have them celebrate annually the fourteenth and fifteenth days of the month of Adar as the time when the Jews got relief from their enemies, and as the month when their sorrow was turned into joy and their mourning into a day of celebration. He wrote them to observe the days as days of feasting and joy and giving presents of food to one another and gifts to the poor. (Esther 9:20–22)

> When they saw the star, they were overjoyed. On coming to the house, they saw the child with his mother Mary, and they bowed down and worshiped him. Then they opened their treasures and presented him with gifts of gold and of incense and of myrrh. (Matthew 2:10–11)

God, of course, gave the greatest gift of all: His love wrapped up in His Son, Jesus. God's love changes everything and everyone it touches. It protects and breathes life and purpose into every minute of every day. God's love is a gift beyond measure that surrounds us and covers us when the fires of life rain down.

I love the story of a man who came home, picked up the paper, and settled into his favorite chair for a few precious and well-deserved moments of solitude after a long day at work. He had just begun to relax when his son burst through the front door. Spotting his dad, the little boy raced across the room, flung himself against his father's knees and said, "Daddy, I love you!" The father gave him a pat on the head and said rather absentmindedly, "Yes, son, I love you too."

Once again, after picking up his paper, the father continued reading, but the boy was not satisfied. He leaned a little farther into the newspaper barricade and said, "But, Daddy, I really, really love you." The man took a deep breath, put down the paper, hugged the boy, and said, "Yes, son. I love you just as much." Again, the dad picked up the paper and resumed reading.

Finally, the little boy could not stand it any longer. He jumped up on his father's lap, crushing the newspaper and any thoughts of relaxation the dad might have had. "Son, what is it that you want?" the tired father asked. In response, the boy threw his arms around his dad and gave him a big squeeze, explaining, "I love you so much, Daddy, and I've just got to *do* something about it!"

That is exactly what God said to Jesus. *Son, I love them so much that I have to* do *something about it!* God defined His unconditional and relentless love for us when He asked His only Son to come to earth as a baby, to live and die for you and for me. And Jesus said, *Yes!* What an indescribable gift! The love of God for you and for me compelled Jesus Christ to willingly exchange a throne for a manger, divinity for humanity and heaven for earth.

God's love is an unconditional love—a love with no strings attached and a gift that breathes life and joy and celebration into every moment of every day. Jesus came, at the request of God, spelling Himself out in a language you and I can understand—a message of love that exists to give.

> Then God made you alive with Christ, for he forgave all our sins. He canceled the record of the charges against us and took it away by nailing it to the cross. (Colossians 2:13–14, NLT)

There is no condemnation for those who are in Christ Jesus. He adores you, girlfriend, just as you are. He wants to spend time with you, laugh with you, dry your tears, and fill your heart with new dreams. Today, no matter where you are or where you have been, He stands waiting for you. Come to Him. Accept Him. No matter how ugly the sin or how great the failure, He loves you. Come to His love. Receive His gift of life and celebrate God, the giver of every good and perfect gift!

Let's Pray

Father, I confess that I often fail to recognize the truth that every good gift comes from Your hand. I pray Your Holy Spirit would give me a fresh awareness and a thankful heart for the very life You freely give me each day and for the gift of eternal life You so freely offer. Help me to see Your hand in the smallest details of my world and teach me to celebrate life each and every day. Thank You for Your faithfulness to me and for Your unfailing love that sustains every step I take. I want to live a life that truly celebrates You! In Jesus's name, amen.

Day 5

My Song

Gwen Smith

Today's Truth

For the Lord God is my strength and my song, and he has become my salvation. (Isaiah 12:2, esv)

Friend to Friend

Just try to keep my daughter from singing. Go ahead and try. You will fail. She must sing. It's just her thing. Some days when I'm writing, or simply trying to piece together a coherent thought, I dream that she could travel to a land far, far away from me and hang out in a soundproof room. *Shhhhhhh! Embrace "quiet" already, girl.* I know. When it comes to 24/7 musical expressions, "Mother of the Year" I am not. And I'm okay with that.

The irony, of course, is that I too love to sing—just not *all* day *every* day like my daughter, and certainly not when I'm writing. Oh, but I do love music. It's central to who I am as a person. I love writing songs, singing songs, learning songs, and playing songs. If my iTunes library were in book form, it would fill the Library of Congress. In many ways my life is processed through melody and verse. And I can scarcely pick up my Bible and spend time in God's presence without having to run to the piano in responsive worship. When His deep calls out to my deep, I just have to chase it musically!

Why?

What is the big deal about songs?

I could never hope to understand the full scope of the answer, but I know this: music is powerful. It heightens our emotions and allows us to feel our way through a thought. Think back to the first time you heard Judy Garland sing "Over the Rainbow"...or Darlene Zschech singing "Shout to the Lord"...or Ray Charles singing "Georgia on My Mind"...or Gloria and Bill Gaither singing "Because He Lives"...or Aretha Franklin singing "Respect"... or Celine Dion singing "My Heart Will Go On"...or Chris Tomlin singing "How Great Is Our God." Pure melodic magic. Notes strung together in excellence can raise us to our feet or push us to our knees.

Because music touches something at the core of our being, it should come as no surprise that one of the names of God found in Scripture is My Song. First seen in Exodus 15, My Song is a name that Moses used to describe God as he celebrated the miraculous deliverance of the Israelites from Egypt. Can you imagine how his heart swelled as he watched God turn a massive body of water into a walking trail for millions of Israelites?

So Moses and his people threw down a big ol' God party on the victory side of the Red Sea!

> Then Moses and the people of Israel sang this song to the
> LORD, saying,
> "I will sing to the LORD, for he has triumphed gloriously;
> the horse and his rider he has thrown into the sea.

The Lord is my strength and my song,
  and he has become my salvation;
this is my God, and I will praise him,
  my father's God, and I will exalt him."
    (Exodus 15:1–2, ESV)

Moses had to sing because his heart couldn't contain the gratitude and awe he felt for God. He called the Lord "My Song." He felt compelled to worship. I totally get that. God had freed His people through a medley of miracle after miracle. How could they *not* respond in grateful worship? How could He not be their Song?

How could He not be ours as well?

The greatest commandment of God to His people is not vague. It is crystal clear. Both the Old and New Testaments tell us that the most vital calling in life—your greatest purpose—is to "'love the Lord your God with all your heart and with all your soul and with all your mind.' This is the first and greatest commandment" (Matthew 22:37–38).

Bam! That's it. What better way for us to express love to God than by living out a life that sings His praise and features Him as the ultimate object of our desire?

In Psalm 40:3, King David expressed God's loving deliverance this way, "He put a new song in my mouth, a hymn of praise to our God. Many will see and fear and put their trust in the Lord."

Other psalms and Old Testament writings reflect this vernacular as well:

By day the Lord directs his love, at night his song is with me—a prayer to the God of my life. (Psalm 42:8)

The LORD is my strength and my song; he has become my salvation. (Psalm 118:14)

Surely God is my salvation; I will trust and not be afraid. The LORD, the LORD, is my strength and my song; he has become my salvation. (Isaiah 12:2)

There's a stanza of an inspired old poem called "The Life That Counts" that speaks to this beautifully.

The life that counts must hopeful be;
In darkest night make melody;
Must wait the dawn on bended knee—
This is the life that counts.[50]

I really want to live a life that counts. Don't you?

I will be the first to admit that my feeble attempts to live out the greatest commandment fall short every single day. I want to love Him perfectly, but I'm just not able to. I want to love Him with all my heart, soul, and mind. Sincerely. But the reality is I can't because I am a distracted worshiper.

My life is busy with ordinary. The laundry never ends, the family activities never cease, dust dominates, and dishes fill my kitchen sink, even when I've just cleared it out. To sprinkle special on our ordinary days, we add music. We sing. We dance. We worship.

So, as much as my daughter's constant melodious outbursts may wear me out, maybe she is on to something after all. If God is our song, then how can we not sing? How can we not find a song—our Song, God—in both the mundane and the miraculous of our lives? If He is our song, then let's raise our voices with His praise!

I love this particular name of God so much that I wrote a song about it with my friend Jourdan Johnson. Read the lyric below as a prayer. Read it out loud. Reflect on His goodness. Then swing over to our Girlfriends in God website to hear the song: www.girlfriendsingod.com/2012/my-strength-my-song/.

My Strength, My Song

Words and music by Jourdan Johnson and Gwen Smith

You speak to my weakness
You tell me Your grace is strength
Your power is made alive in me

You're near in my waiting
You hear every prayer I breathe
You raise me up from the miry clay

So I stand upon the Rock, Jesus...

My Strength, my Song
I trust You in all things
For You are faithful
I will follow where You lead
My Strength, my Song
My Strength, my Song

You call me to healing
You promise to never leave
You take me beyond my doubt and fear

You save with compassion
Rejoice over me and sing
You quiet me with Your endless love

So I come with confidence, Jesus...

You are the God of all hope
You're my strong foundation
You are my Fortress and help
I will not be shaken

And so we end with a song. How perfectly beautiful! Sharon, Mary, and I pray that you will feel compelled to sing to the Lord heartfelt praises because, through our time together in this devotional study, you now know Him better by name.

> Those who know your name will trust in
> you, for you, LORD, have never forsaken
> those who seek you. (Psalm 9:10)

Let's Pray

Dear Lord, You are my Strength and my Song. Thank You for giving us music! Thank You for inviting me to honor You in praise with instruments, voices, verses, and melodies. Help me to love You with my heart, mind, and soul...more today than yesterday...more tomorrow than today...and more the next day than tomorrow. In Jesus's name, amen.

Now It's Your Turn

Time for Reflection

- In this chapter, Sharon introduced us to the God of Glory and shared that God's glory is how He makes His presence known. How has God revealed a glimpse of His glory in your life? Can you describe a moment of sudden glory when you knew without a doubt that you had experienced the Divine in your daily life?
- When we live and walk in union with God, we will see moments of sudden glory throughout our day. Describe what it means to "live and move and have [your] being" in Christ (Acts 17:28).
- "Love the Lord your God with all your heart and with all your soul and with all your mind" (Matthew 22:37). What does this statement indicate about how God wants you to commune and communicate with Him? What does it imply about how God wants to commune and communicate with you? Consider and discuss.
- This week, we also looked at God as our Portion and were reminded that when we seek Him first, He takes care of our needs (Matthew 6:25–34). How has God met your needs in the past? Think of at least one instance. Do you trust that He is able to meet your needs today? Why or why not?

- How would our prayer lives be different if we asked for more of God rather than more of His gifts—if we seek God *as* the answer instead of *for* the answer?
- Read and consider these verses: "As the deer pants for streams of water, so my soul pants for you, O God. My soul thirsts for God, for the living God" (Psalm 42:1–2). On a scale of 0 to 5, how would you rank your soul thirst for God?

  0 = God who?

  1 = Parched… "I Can't Get No Satisfaction" has been my theme song lately.

  2 = Cotton mouth… If I could get beyond my distractions and frustrations, I might have time to think about seeking God more.

  3 = Between sips… My thirst varies. At times, I'm satisfied. At times, I long for another taste.

  4 = Big-time thirsty… Fully aware of my need. Fully aware of His goodness.

  5 = Hook me up to an IV… I'm all in! I'm as thirsty as they come! Bring. It. On.
- Read this prayer by King Hezekiah: "O Lord, God of Israel, enthroned between the cherubim, you alone are God over all the kingdoms of the earth. You have made heaven and earth. Give ear, O Lord, and hear; open your eyes, O Lord, and see; listen to the words Sennacherib has sent to insult the living God. It is true, O Lord, that the Assyrian kings have laid waste these nations and their lands. They have thrown their gods into the fire and destroyed them, for they were not gods but only wood and stone, fashioned by men's hands. Now, O Lord our God, deliver us from his hand, so that all kingdoms on earth may know that you alone, O Lord, are God" (2 Kings 19:15–19).

What does Hezekiah's prayer reveal about his understanding of the "living God"?

Hezekiah prayed for deliverance, but what was his ultimate hoped-for outcome?

How can his prayer be a model for our own prayers?

- Look up and read Daniel 6:25–27. After King Darius looked into the lions' den and saw Daniel sitting with his furry friends, unscathed, what did he call God?
- Daniel's faith led him to a lions' den. *Scary!* Sometimes our faith leads us to scary places too. God's deliverance often shines the brightest when circumstances are the darkest. Can you think of a time when God showed up and showed off in your life in such an undeniable way that it led others to consider that ours is the living God?
- James 1 tells us that every perfect gift is from God, the giver of good gifts. He's so amazing that way! For fun: What is one of the best gifts you have ever been given? (Besides salvation. *Smiles.* Go girlfriend on this one!)
- Can you think of a time when God gave you a surprise gift? Give some scoop and give Him glory!
- Our final devotion of the book features God as our Song. First seen in the Bible as a term of affection used by Moses in celebration of the deliverance he and the Israelites experienced at the shores of the Red Sea, the name My Song resurfaces several times in the psalms. If you had to pick a song that captured your feelings for God today, what would it be?
- Wrap up your response time with prayer. Move from confession, to adoration, to thanksgiving, and end with your petitions (personal prayer needs).

Going Deeper with God

List: the attributes and names of God with their meanings that were covered this week.

1. ______________________________
2. ______________________________
3. ______________________________
4. ______________________________
5. ______________________________

Read: Daniel 6

Worship as you **listen** and **reflect:** Find inspiration in a song Gwen co-wrote called "My Strength, My Song." Find it here: www.girlfriendsingod.com/2012/my-strength-my-song/.

Your GiG *Knowing God by Name* Journal

Spend a few moments contemplating and journaling about some of the scriptural truths that moved your heart as you read the devotions this week. Then use the space below to collect your thoughts or write a prayer of response to God.

____

____

____

____

____

____

4-28-16

Ronda Threadgill - melanoma

Janet - knee surgery - doing well

Helen & John Rambo

Baby Dominic

Barbie Barton

JoAnn Hood

Brenda Barger in-laws

Jillian

Kendall

Kristen - in-vitro fertilization

Ashley - delivery

For the LORD GOD is my strength and my song,
and he has become my salvation. (Isaiah 12:2, ESV)

Acknowledgments

We would like to thank the many men and women who made this book possible:

Bill Jensen, our guy-friend in God who dusts off his pompoms and cheers us on.

Laura Barker and the WaterBrook Multnomah team, who believed in our project and took us under their Random House wing.

Our husbands, Steve, Brad, and Dan, who put up with our stacks of paper, late-night writing, and repeated requests of "Honey, can you read this and tell me what you think?"

Crosswalk.com, which debuted our Girlfriends in God devotions many years ago and continues to allow us to minister to women around the globe.

BibleGateway.com, which has also locked arms with us to share the hope and healing of Jesus Christ.

Our heavenly Father who equips us, our Savior Jesus who envelops us, and the precious Holy Spirit who empowers us.

Pronunciation Guide

Abba	AH-bah
Adonai	ah-doh-NAH-ee
Agape	ah-GAH-pay
Atik Yomin	ah-TEEK YOH-meen
Basileus basileōn	bah-sil-YOOCE bah-sil-ay-OWN
Chelqi	khel-KEE
Elohim	eh-lo-HEEM
El Chay	el CHAY
El Elyon	el el-YONE
El Hanne'eman	el hah-NAY-eh-mahn
El Kannah	el kah-NAH
El Kahvohd	el kaw-BODE
El Olam	el oh-LAM
El Roi	el raw-EE
El Sali	el sah-LEE
El Shaddai	el shah-DIE-ee
Haggo'el	hah-go-EL
Ish	EESH
Migdal Oz	mig-dahl OHZ
Miqweh Yisrael	MIK-veh yis-rah-EL
Paraklesis	pah-RAH-klay-sis

Yahweh	yah-WEH
Yahweh El Ashiyb	yah-WEH el ah-SHEEB
Yahweh Hesed	yah-WEH KHEH-sed
Yahweh M'Kaddesh	yah-WEH KAW-dash
Yahweh Nissi	yah-WEH nih-SEE
Yahweh Rapha	yah-WEH roh-FEH
Yahweh Rohi	yah-WEH roh-EE
Yahweh Shalom	yah-WEH shah-LOME
Yahweh Shammah	yah-WEH SHA-mah
Yahweh Tsidkenu	yah-WEH tsid-KAY-noo
Yahweh Tsuri	yah-WEH tsoo-REE
Yahweh Yireh	yah-WEH yee-REH
Yatsar	yaw-TSAR
Ysuah	YEH-shoo-ah

NOTES

1. Kenneth L. Barker, gen. ed., *The NIV Study Bible,* 1984 ed. (Grand Rapids, MI: Zondervan, 1985), note on Genesis 17:15–16.
2. Bruce Marchiano, *Jesus, the Man Who Loved Women: He Treasures, Esteems, and Delights in You* (New York: Howard Books, 2008), 31.
3. Carolyn Custis James, *When Life and Beliefs Collide: How Knowing God Makes a Difference* (Grand Rapids, MI: Zondervan, 2002), 177.
4. William D. Mounce, gen. ed., *Mounce's Complete Expository Dictionary of Old and New Testament Words* (Grand Rapids, MI: Zondervan, 2006), 450.
5. John J. Parsons, "The Hebrew Name of God—El," Hebrew for Christians, www.hebrew4christians.com/Names_of_G-d/El/el.html.
6. Spiros Zodhiates, *The Complete Word Study Old Testament* (Chattanooga, TN: AMG, 2004), 2371.
7. Herbert Lockyer, *All the Divine Names and Titles in the Bible* (Grand Rapids, MI: Zondervan, 1975), 14.
8. William Shakespeare, *Othello,* act 3, scene 3, lines 165–66.
9. Mark Twain, *Letters from the Earth: Uncensored Writings,* ed. Bernard DeVoto (New York: Perennial Classics, 2004), 27.
10. Francis Thompson, "The Hound of Heaven" quoted in *Chapters into Verse: Poetry in English Inspired by the Bible,*

vol. 2, ed. Robert Atwan and Laurance Wieder (New York: Oxford University Press, 1993), 187.

11. Walter A. Elwell and Barry J. Beitzel, *Baker Encyclopedia of the Bible* (Grand Rapids, MI: Baker Book House, 1988), 885.
12. Listen to the song here: www.girlfriendsingod.com/2012/worship-holy-adonai/.
13. "Although God inspired most of the Old Testament books to be written in Hebrew, Daniel and Ezra wrote portions of their books in Aramaic or Syriac, the language spoken throughout the Persian Empire during their time. It had also replaced Hebrew as the language of common speech of the Jews." Martin G. Collins, "The Names of God," Bible Tools, www.bibletools.org/index.cfm/fuseaction/Library.sr/CT/RA/k/367.
14. Hayley DiMarco, *Obsessed: Breaking Free from the Things That Consume You* (Grand Rapids, MI: Revell, 2012).
15. A. W. Tozer, *The Knowledge of the Holy* (New York: HarperCollins, 1961), 1.
16. A. W. Tozer, *That Incredible Christian* (Camp Hill, PA: Christian Publications, 1986).
17. A. T. Robertson, *Word Pictures in the New Testament* (Nashville, TN: Broadman, 1933), Revelation 17:14.
18. Simon J. Kistemaker and William Hendriksen, *Revelation,* New Testament Commentary (Grand Rapids, MI: Baker, 2002), 476.
19. Chad Brand et al., eds., *Holman Illustrated Bible Dictionary* (Nashville, TN: Holman, 2003), 1221.

20. Adapted from Sharon Jaynes, *A Sudden Glory: God's Lavish Response to Your Ache for Something More* (Colorado Springs: Multnomah, 2012), 111.
21. "The Names of God in the Old Testament," Blue Letter Bible, www.blueletterbible.org/study/misc/name_god.cfm.
22. Jean-Pierre de Caussade, quoted in *A Guide to Prayer for All God's People,* ed. Rueben Job and Norman Shawchuck (Nashville, TN: Upper Room, 1990), 244.
23. C. S. Lewis, *God in the Dock* (Grand Rapids, MI: Eerdmans, 1994), 52.
24. Philip Yancey, *Where Is God When It Hurts?,* anniversary ed. (Grand Rapids, MI: Zondervan, 1990, 1977), 161.
25. Adapted from Jaynes, *A Sudden Glory,* 120–21, 123–24.
26. Richard Fuller, quoted in L. B. Cowman, *Streams in the Desert* (Grand Rapids, MI: Zondervan, 1996), April 1.
27. Parsons, "The Hebrew Name of God—El."
28. Parsons, "The Hebrew Name of God—El."
29. Ann Spangler, *The Names of God* (Grand Rapids, MI: Zondervan, 2009), 47.
30. Albert Barnes, "Notes on the Bible," note on Colossians 3:15, www.sacred-texts.com/bib/cmt/barnes/col003.htm.
31. Jim Quillen, *Alcatraz from Inside: The Hard Years, 1942–1952* (San Francisco: Golden Gate National Park Association, 1991), i.
32. "Nature of God," God's Sabbath, www.gods-sabbath.org/pdf-files/60-names-of-God-His-nature-tab.pdf.
33. "Sanctification in the Bible: 1 Peter 1:1–2," Gospel.com, www.gospel.com/bookmarks/Sanctification-Bible-1-Peter-1-1-2/9377.

34. Billy Graham, "A Daily Process," Today's Devotion, October 2, 2009, www.thecove.org/todays-devotion/10-2-2009.
35. Judson Corwall and Stelman Smith, *The Exhaustive Dictionary of Bible Names* (Alachua, FL: Bridge-Logos, 1998), 68.
36. *Mounce's Complete Expository Dictionary,* 348.
37. Adapted from Jaynes, *A Sudden Glory,* 21–22.
38. Peggy Overstreet, "Builder," *Greek Word Studies* (blog), April 3, 2007, http://greekwordstudies.blogspot.com/2007/04/builder.html.
39. Adapted from Sharon Jaynes, *The 5 Dreams of Every Woman…and How God Wants to Fulfill Them* (Eugene, OR: Harvest House, 2004), 13.
40. *Mounce's Complete Expository Dictionary,* 242.
41. J. I. Packer, *Knowing God* (Downers Grove, IL: InterVarsity, 1973), 182.
42. Allan Emery, *A Turtle on a Fencepost: Little Lessons of Large Importance* (Austin, TX: World Wide Publishing, 1980).
43. *The Wiersbe Bible Commentary: New Testament* (Colorado Springs: David C. Cook, 2007), 502.
44. "Integrity," The Jesus Site, www.jesussite.com/quotes/integrity.html.
45. *Mounce's Complete Expository Dictionary,* 289.
46. W. E. Vine, Merrill F. Unger, and William White Jr., *Vine's Complete Expository Dictionary of Old and New Testament Words* (Nashville, TN: Thomas Nelson, 1985), 267.
47. Adapted from Jaynes, *A Sudden Glory,* 8–10.
48. Corwall and Smith, *Exhaustive Dictionary of Bible Names,* 78.

49. Charles H. Spurgeon, *Morning and Evening: Daily Readings,* New Modern Edition (Peabody, MA: Hendrickson, 2006), Morning, November 16.
50. [A.W.S.], "The Life That Counts," *Heart Throbs in Prose and Verse Dear to the American People,* vol. 2, ed. Joe Mitchell Chapple (New York: Grosset & Dunlap, 1911), 6.

ABOUT *Girlfriends* IN GOD

GIRLFRIENDS IN GOD is a nondenominational devotional and conference ministry that crosses generational and racial boundaries to bring the body of Christ together as believers. Just as God sent Ruth to Naomi and Mary to Elizabeth, God continues to use women to encourage and equip other women in their spiritual journeys. Through online daily devotions, conferences, published books, CDs, and music videos, God is using this incredible team of women to bring the hope and healing of Jesus Christ to a hurting world.

GIRLFRIENDS IN GOD conferences are "turnkey" events designed to meet the needs of any ministry, church, or organization desiring to impact the lives of women for Christ. The GIG team helps women experience the height, width, and depth of God's love in a world cloaked in hopelessness and despair. The leadership team of Girlfriends in God is committed to helping women grow deeper in their relationships with God and soar higher in freedom and faith.

The team includes Sharon Jaynes, Gwen Smith, and Mary Southerland.

SHARON JAYNES is an international conference speaker and best-selling author of seventeen books and Bible studies, including *The Power of a Woman's Words, Becoming the Woman of His Dreams,* and *A Sudden Glory: God's Lavish Response to Your Ache for Something More.* Her in-depth knowledge of Scripture, combined with an engaging storytelling style, makes her a favorite at women's events. Sharon's passion is to encourage, equip, and empower women to walk in confidence as they grasp their true identity as children of God and coheirs with Christ. Helping women to live fully and free in Christ is the heartbeat of her ministry. Sharon's books have been translated into many languages such as Spanish, Portuguese, Korean, and Romanian. She is a frequent guest on radio and television programs including *Focus on the Family, Family Life,* and *Revive Our Hearts.* Sharon makes her home in North Carolina with her husband, Steve. They have one grown son, Steven, who uses his writing talents in the marketing/advertising world. To learn more about Sharon's ministry, blog, resources, and online Bible studies, visit www.sharonjaynes.com.

Gwen Smith is wife to Brad and mom to three cool kids: two teens and a tween named Preston, Hunter, and Kennedy. She is also a speaker, worship leader, author, and songwriter whose fun, enthusiastic, and relatable communication style puts audiences at ease and bridges generational, denominational, and racial divides. Her goal is to encourage women to think big thoughts about God by pointing them to His truth and grace through stories, songs, and Scripture. Gwen's inspiring restoration story is featured in her book *Broken into Beautiful,* and has engaged audiences across the world, including through appearances on *Life Today* and *The 700 Club.* She knows the power of redemption and delivers a compelling message of hope to thousands each year at conferences, concerts, and events. To learn more, visit www.gwensmith.net. Connect with her via social media at www.Facebook.com/GwenSmithMusic or tweet with her here: @GwenSmithMusic.

Mary Southerland is an international speaker and a dynamic communicator, delivering a powerful message that changes lives.

Through warmth, humor, transparency, and solid biblical teaching, Mary leads women to discover the powerful truth of God's Word and motivates them to apply it in their daily lives. Mary's books include *Hope in the Midst of Depression, Sandpaper People, Escaping the Stress Trap, Experiencing God's Power in Your Ministry,* and *Trusting God.* One of Mary's greatest pleasures is serving beside her husband, Dan, who is the lead teaching pastor at Westside Family Church in Lenexa, Kansas. Mary relishes her ministry as a pastor's wife, a mother to their two children, Jered and Danna, and "Mimi" to her five grandchildren. To learn more about Mary's ministry, resources, and online Bible studies, visit www.marysoutherland.com.

These three women have joined together to bring you inspirational devotions and conferences that will change your life. No matter where you are on your journey toward the heart of God, Girlfriends in God will help you take the next step closer.

To learn more about Girlfriends in God, to sign up for their free daily e-devotions, or to inquire about hosting a Girlfriends in God conference, visit www.girlfriendsingod.com or write to:

Girlfriends in God
PO Box 725
Matthews, NC 28106

God Doesn't Want You to *Do More*—He *Wants You*

Do you long for something more in your relationship with God? The good news is that *something more* does not mean *doing more.* In fact, the real question is not "What does God want from you?" but "What does God want for you?"

Read a chapter excerpt at www.WaterBrookMultnomah.com!